But They Look So Happy

Xanti Bootcov

Copyright 2018 by Xanti Bootcov

First published by Joanne Fedler Media 2018

www.joannefedler.com (publisher's website)
www.marketingmentor.live (design by Nailia Minnebaeva)

All rights reserved. No part of this publication may be reproduced, stored in a retrieval system or transmitted in any form or by any means, electronic, mechanical photocopying, recording or otherwise without the prior written permission of the author. Printed in Australia, South Africa, UK and USA.

National Library of Australia Cataloguing-in-Publication data:

ISBN 978-1-925842-06-7 (Paperback)
ISBN 978-1-925842-05-0 (Hardback)
ISBN 978-1-925842-07-4 (E-book)

*I would like to dedicate this book to the real Miguel and Isaak,
and all the other brave children like them who are striving to survive.
You are braver than you know.*

Contents

Preface	7
Mexico City	11
Chapter 1: The Man in the Grey Truck	13
Chapter 2: Back Before We Go Forward	18
Chapter 3: Living Under Down Under	21
Chapter 4: Around the World	25
Chapter 5: Meeting Strangers	28
Chapter 6: Little by Little	32
Chapter 7: Yes, You Can – No, You Can't	41
Chapter 8: Oliver Guantanamo	48
Chapter 9: The Duck Plan	51
Chapter 10: Unfamiliar Road Home	61
Chapter 11: The Broken Promise	64
Chapter 12: Feelings	71
Chapter 13: The Powers That Be	78
Chapter 14: Music Tames the Beast	84
Chapter 15: The Sleeping Game	91
Chapter 16: Swim, Said the Mama Fishie	96
Chapter 17: Chocolates: A Weapon of Choice	99
Chapter 18: African Game	104
Chapter 19: The Silence	107
Chapter 20: Big in Japan	111
Chapter 21: Without Brakes	114
Chapter 22: Not My Mexico	117

London   123
Chapter 23: School and Snow   125
Chapter 24: Different Agendas   128
Chapter 25: Harry Potter and the Elusive Scones   135
Chapter 26: A Cry for Help   139
Chapter 27: The Unwanted   145
Chapter 28: Trains, Planes and Automobiles   150
Chapter 29: London's Burning   156

Sydney   163
Chapter 30: Living with Family   165
Chapter 31: Jekyll and Hyde   170
Chapter 32: Hard Work Makes Dreams Come True   176
Chapter 33: In Theory   181
Chapter 34: My Brother's Keeper   185
Chapter 35: Oh Child of Mine   189
Chapter 36: Fire Fire   195
Chapter 37: Trapped   198
Chapter 38: Drink, Drank, Drunk   204
Chapter 39: Future Shock   210
Chapter 40: School's Out   214
Chapter 41: Winning and Losing   222
Chapter 42: After Holiday Blues   226
Chapter 43: Misconceptions and Other Realities   230
Chapter 44: Somewhere to Run   236
Chapter 45: I'm Okay – You're Okay?   239
Chapter 46: Who Are Miguel and Isaak?   244
Chapter 47: Finding Myself   248

My Son's Thoughts After Reading the Book   259
Acknowledgements   263
About the Author   265

Preface

Perspective is a funny thing. A story will not present itself in the same way to each of us. As time goes by, even our own memories of the past may change.

What I remember is that I moved to Mexico with a boyfriend, the Engineer. On our way through our lives, we met and then adopted two of the most interesting six-year-old boys. Together, we experienced one garden fire, one house fire and two cars burning out. We travelled across the world and explored many new countries.

As a family, each of us had distinct opinions on what parenthood meant. To the adults, it was about providing a loving, secure and kind home. It meant guiding our children and giving them options for a bright future. Our children, who'd had a challenging start in life, found this threatening. Our views conflicted. This split our family down the middle. We became a divided group of *us and them*. Parents in one group, children in another.

This type of conflict can pull families together or push them apart.

My story is about how we managed to find an equilibrium that almost broke us. I don't wish to discourage anyone from adopting a child. Children are precious and need protection. They should be given a gentle life wherever possible. I tried to make my love conquer all and to get my boys the help I believed would make their lives easier. But my children did not understand or trust soft love. It made their lives feel tenuous, so a more difficult road had to be taken. Through it all, we are still clinging to a thread that binds us together. At times, the thread is tenuous; at times, it feels a bit stronger. Sometimes I think it is stretched to the point that it will snap and send us hurtling in different directions.

This story is mine and not my children's. I first started writing this book just for myself. I wanted to better understand what had happened to us and to acknowledge the part I had played in my family's struggle. I wanted to give my experience voice and shape. As I wrote, I met others who were going through similar family dynamics and were also looking for answers. When I told them my story, they said it gave them a little bit of peace. Knowing that we had gone through a challenging time seemed to help others feel less alone. My story gave them strength. I soon found that my reason for writing this book had changed. After a discussion with my sons, they liked the idea of our story helping others.

Nothing in this book is made up, although I have appropriated some scenes from other families who have been in similar situations. I have based it on the emotions and memories of my experience. To further protect my sons, I have changed their names. In some cases, I have switched events around or attributed personality traits to a different character in the book. Miguel and Isaak are not direct representations of my sons. They are an aggregate of my children and a few other children we have met along the way. At times, I have over-dramatised a scene to underscore the emotions that were at play. I have been deliberately vague with some details which I judged to be less important than conveying the emotional truth of the situation.

Strong emotions are the singular constant for most of the families to whom I have spoken. Being engulfed in overwhelming feelings of failure can lead us to believe we should have done better. I would like to impress upon readers that they can trust everything about themselves, including that feeling of failure. The important lesson of failure is how we choose to deal with it.

This book is not the answer. It does not try to give advice. It is simply a true story.

Mexico City

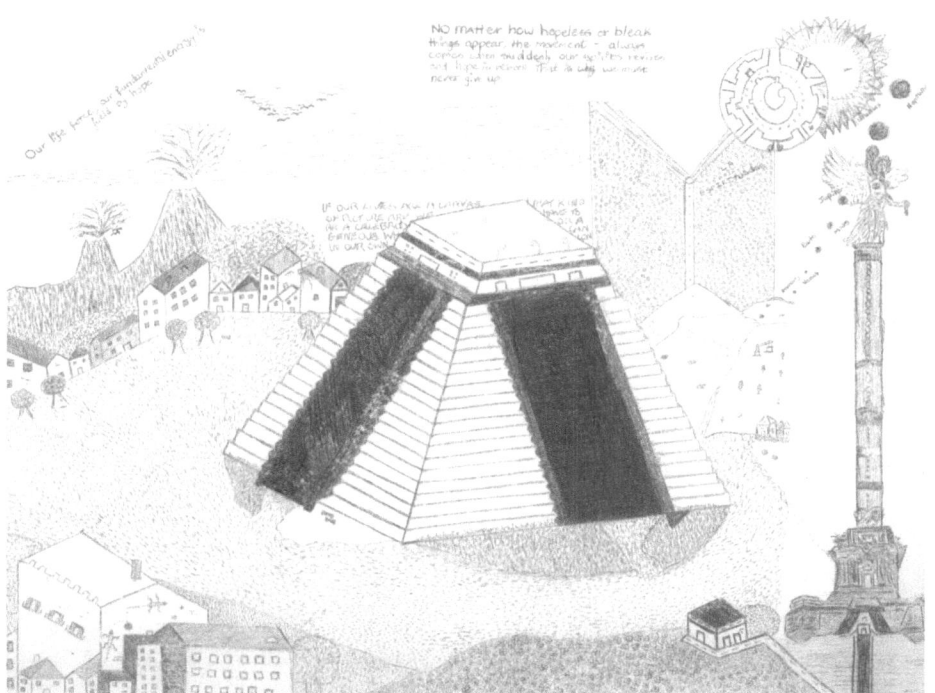

CHAPTER 1
The Man in the Grey Truck

It took five police cars to escort us like criminals to the police station in the centre of Mexico City.

It was the 5th of September. The Engineer and I had started the day with a slow race into the city to buy two pairs of kids' Converse shoes. The traffic was particularly chaotic closer to the Zocalo, where the local market had thrived since the days of the Aztec.

We were not far from the parking lot when a man driving a grey truck covered in dust overtook us and then blocked our way.

'I wonder what that is all about,' the Engineer said, as he slowly manoeuvred the car around him. The driver frowned at us through bushy eyebrows.

'He's calling the policeman standing on the corner,' I answered, leaning out the window to see what was going on. I'd skipped breakfast and had been hoping we would have time to get an empanada from the food stand around the corner. The man in the grey truck was gesticulating furiously.

As we slowed to turn into the parking lot, I noticed the policeman with his flamboyant uniform walking nonchalantly towards us, licking his lips. He knocked on the car window.

'Driver's licence, señor.' He looked like a model with his oblong Ray-Bans.

'What is the problem, officer?' The Engineer carefully showed his driver's licence through the barely opened window. We'd lived in Mexico long enough to be familiar with the prevalence of fabricated traffic violations. It had been a cultural practice since the days when policemen collected money for the Viceroy's false teeth. The familiarly used phrase for this was 'mordida', which means 'bite': a bite out of your wallet.

'Show me your driver's licence.' The policeman distributed his weight evenly between widespread feet and rested his hands on his belt.

'What have I done?' The Engineer held on to his licence. He knew that once the officer had it in his hands, we would be ensnared.

'You committed an infraction. Driver's licence, por favor.'

By now a few more uniforms had gathered around our car. One of them was pointing to the two six-year-old boys.

'Get out, señor. The rest of you stay in the car, por favor.' I got the feeling Oblong-glasses was working out how big a bunch of flowers this mordida would buy his wife.

As the Engineer got out the car, the man in the grey truck could no longer hold himself back. He got out of his truck and walked over until he was standing nose to nose with the Engineer, his potbelly peeking out from under a T-shirt that had once been white.

'Hey, I'm the guy who called the poli on you, güey,' he swore. As he spoke, his moustache flapped over his bottom lip. 'I won't let you get away with this,' he proudly said, as if he was a hero. He had a big smile on his sweaty face.

Uniformed men began shouting questions through the open windows to the two kids sitting in our car.

'Do you know these people?' one uniform shouted towards the back seat. He removed his gloves.

'Where do you live?' another yelled into the car.

'What are you doing with these gueros?' bellowed a third.

'Guys, be calm and just answer the nice poli,' I said softly.

'Señora, we are not talking to you. Be quiet.'

When I'm scared, my mind becomes focused and calm, but I was worried about the children in the back. *Our* children. Our *Mexican* children. Our *adopted* Mexican children.

'These are my parents,' Isaak said as he looked the uniforms straight on.

Most of the time Isaak was dazed, quiet. But in this situation, he was awake. Alert. In form. Alive. Miguel, usually the angry one, had been stunned into silence.

'How can they be your parents? Where are they taking you?' The questions shot out and the answers created more confusion.

Outside the car, the Engineer struggled to stay on his feet as the policemen began to push and shove him. The conversation was going too fast for me to pick up anything but the expletives I'd learnt.

'I want Los Derechos Humanos,' the Engineer said as he adjusted his clothes and took a deep breath. Silence exploded around us. He had used the golden words. The human rights representatives were the only ones the cops were afraid of.

'If you want them, señor, we have to take you to the station,' Oblong-glasses said as the aggression left him.

'I'm okay with that. I think that my human rights are being violated, so I want Los Derechos Humanos,' the Engineer said, loudly enough for the onlookers to hear.

'We'll have to escort you, señor,' Oblong-glasses said as he waved goodbye to his wife's flowers.

As the blue lights chaperoned us and we drove, I noticed a dirty street child on the side of the road wipe her nose on her faded purple sleeve. Pollution hung in the air. Life went on for other people as I held my breath and wondered how this was going to unfold.

'Don't give them an excuse to ratchet up the situation,' I said. 'We know that according to the Mexican constitution, residents have rights and we have done nothing wrong. We need to get through the next few minutes together. Calmly. We can't allow them to separate us while they decide what to do. Just stay composed.' I was talking in Spanish so the boys could understand but I was speaking to the Engineer. I saw his shoulders relax.

'I know,' he said, 'but they think we've kidnapped the boys.'

'This must be how black kids in the US feel when the cops stop them randomly,' I remarked.

We had switched to English, not wanting the boys to fear the prospect of us being arrested.

'We need to show respect and be flexible,' I continued. 'Our rights won't mean a thing if we give them an excuse to arrest us.' I was worried that something could happen to the boys during the time it would take to reverse a false arrest.

Blue lights flashed. Hawkers watched, hoping we would make a break for it. Tourists, confused by the kerfuffle, huddled around whispering. Street kids pointed to the two children sitting on the back seat of our car. We drove in silence the rest of the way with the police escorting us. As we approached the police station, we had no idea what would happen next – in Mexico, these scenarios were unpredictable. But one thing we knew for sure was that after all we'd been through to get them, we would do anything – and I mean anything – to protect our boys.

Since we'd adopted Miguel and Isaak, we'd discovered a resilience we had not needed before. It had been a slow and arduous process. I knew that we needed to draw on inner strength and adaptability to get us through the next hour. Once again, we were about to be cross-examined regarding the origin of our family. Even though the courts had finally declared us kin, we were never allowed to forget, not even for one moment, that we were not a naturally born family. Trivialities such as going to the shops, finding a school or walking in the parks – even buying shoes – would never be simple for us again.

We had had no idea how many challenges these adoptions would put in our path. We had thought it would be easy because, for one thing, the Engineer and I were not adoption virgins. He and his sister were both adopted. As a child, I had fallen for the common adoption tale. I lied to my friends and told them that *I* was adopted. I loved the idea that Mummy and Daddy had chosen me out of all the little children in the world. It didn't matter to me that my sisters and I had an undeniably common look, and I had a place in the family I was born into. I had many friends and some cousins who were adopted too. With our collective adoption experience, we thought that we knew what we were doing. We thought we could rescue our children, and they would learn to love and trust and be safe.

We were wrong.

CHAPTER 2

Back Before We Go Forward

To explain how a South African couple was nearly arrested in Mexico City, I need to go back to an earlier beginning.

Soon after I met the Engineer, we found ourselves sitting among friends, debating the controversial topics of adoption and abortion.

'I don't know what I'd do if I had an unplanned pregnancy and was confronted with the choice, but I'd want to make the decision myself. I wouldn't want my government or closest religious outlet to decide for me.' I sounded like a zealot. 'Besides, I don't think adoption works.' I blurted this last out, conveniently overlooking my own desire to have been adopted.

'Why not?' the Engineer asked, his smiling blue eyes laughing.

'Well, how would *you* like to be told that you were not good enough for your mother to keep you?' I asked.

'I was a baby when I was adopted, and I've always known,' he said. 'It's never been a problem.'

I hadn't known that he was adopted, and my cynical mouth had embarrassed me. Now there was no way out of what I had just said. I'd seen him with his parents. I'd witnessed the love between them and was confident he'd had a secure and stable upbringing. In that moment, the Engineer was having fun with my discomfort, amused by my sudden realisation that our friends were horrified at my cluelessness.

Engineers are born engineers. It doesn't matter what environment they grow up in; they can't help following their true nature. My engineer, like the rest of them, was born to be just that. His father was a butcher and his mother worked as an office administrator, but from a young age he loved taking things apart and playing with walkie-talkies. Just like most engineers, there's not a lot he can't create if he sets his eccentric mind to it. In my experience, all engineers are oddballs who use a diverse code of thought, always looking for levers and algorithms to effect change. Simply put, engineers are from Mars and the rest of us? Well, we're from Earth.

Mine is a farm boy at heart and a city boy by default. His hippie clothes belie his energy. Although he is comfortable in the world, like me, he enjoys being on his own. When I think of him, I hear computer keys clicking away. I feel the wind and the quiet stillness and dependency of the earth. These are the elements of his nature. He is as at ease stepping off a cliff with his paraglider as he is diving into the deep blue sea with his scuba gear. He is an adventurer, and together, we go into the great beyond. Engineers can do anything, and I always knew mine would do just that for me.

I didn't grow up playing with dolls much, and neither did I gravitate to the idea of looking after small, chubby humans. This disinterest in baby caring signalled the downfall of my relationship with an aunt who hoped I'd provide entertainment at her child's birthday party. But that was more my cousin's style. Not only was she happy entertaining them, the kids flocked to her. She told stories and made them laugh. I, on the other hand, didn't know what to do. I would stand in front of them, looking at their bright, expectant faces, and freeze. It was clear to me, even then, that my cousin was gifted with the soft, mothering touch.

By the time I was ten years old, my first baby arrived. She was a fluffy ginger miniature Pomeranian called Mandy. The day before she died, we argued while I tried to change her tick-and-flea collar. I knew that she didn't like me tugging at her neck, but even at that age I understood that mothers needed to be tough so that their children would be safe. The next morning, while I was learning Afrikaans at school, Mandy was run over by a truck.

When I became a young adult I worked in a recreational art centre teaching kids arts and crafts during the school holidays, but I still wasn't longing to produce my own little descendants. I had no yearning to be pregnant. Although I did enjoy the interaction with these little creative minds, I wanted to travel the world with nothing to hinder me. On the odd occasion when I thought about becoming a mother, I always imagined my children lying next to me, loving me. This was unquestionable – a given.

People are often shocked when they hear that I was not dying to have kids or that the Engineer didn't long to be a father. But once we met our children and once we made the decision to become parents, we were fully committed to them. There would be nothing we wouldn't do for them.

CHAPTER 3

Living Under Down Under

When I was twenty-one, I followed the ubiquitous 'love of my life' to live in the USA. He was everything I thought I wanted and needed, but love was not enough to safeguard our relationship. I had to walk away. In some ways, I never got over it, and the complicated emotions that refused to die taught me I could be strong. I had to remind myself of this when I became a mother. But as a parent, your commitment to your children is about much more than love. I could walk away from him and all that the relationship entailed, but I could never walk away from my children.

I had always been open to new surroundings, but when I moved to New Zealand, I experienced culture shock – it was a little too quiet. The Engineer and I decided to buy a motorbike. I knew that my father, ever worried about his daughters, wouldn't approve. When we were kids, getting on a motorbike was one of four things he had forbidden. The other three were ear piercing ('It's painful and you'll get infected'), horse riding ('You'll fall off and break something') and skydiving ('You'll land wrong and break your neck').

For the most part, as a child, I tried to listen to my parents and not disappoint them, but I confess that with the help of my mother, who absorbed the brunt of the ensuing arguments, I pierced my ears and went horseback riding.

Hoping that my father, who was in South Africa, around 11,757 km away, wouldn't find out about my motorbike adventure, I decided I could do this. We would buy a motorbike. I would call it Blue and I would feel the wind on my face and freedom in my heart.

But of course, it wasn't that simple. I had never learnt to ride so much as a bicycle – which was surprising because my parents owned a hardware shop. From a young age, I helped sell bicycles to customers who wanted to surprise their kids with birthday presents. I listened to all the cycling tips. I learnt how to choose a bike. Most importantly, I learnt how to teach kids to ride. But I didn't learn how to ride one myself.

I was about nine years old when, one Saturday after 'work', I brought home a shiny new bicycle. I remember riding it around our big round dining room table despite our very large front lawn, side garden and huge backyard. I felt more secure riding indoors. I was still using the training wheels when, on the second day, I took the bike for a quick spin around the dining room table. The back wheel fell off. Back to the shop it went. And it was never seen again. Later, when I had my own children, and the wheels really came off in my life, I would reflect on this story.

So before I could ride Blue, I had to *learn* to ride Blue. In New Zealand, you have to pass a proficiency test in order to get your learner biker's licence. I nervously called the instructor and explained that I wanted to book in for my learner's proficiency test.

'I've never ridden a bike before,' I told him.

'No worries,' he said. 'I'll show you everything you need to know.'

On the great day, I eagerly stood listening to the instructor.

'So to sum up: if you know how to drive a manual car, there is no trick to changing gears. It's simply the reverse. Your hands do the legwork and your feet do the handwork.'

'But how do you *ride* the bike?' I asked, perplexed.

I watched the instructor (unsuccessfully) try not to roll his eyes at me. He went over the instructions again, reminding me that he had just told me all of this, but he was happy to go over it again if I needed him to. It was cold, and we both wanted to get started as soon as possible.

'No, no,' I said. 'I understand the gears. I just don't know how to ride. You know, balance on the bike.'

'Aahh,' he said, relieved. 'It's just like a pushbike.'

'But I've never been on a scooter before,' I said, assuming pushbike was Kiwi for scooter.

'No worries,' he said. 'Just think of this as a pushbike rather than a scooter.'

Exasperated, I asked, 'But what is a pushbike?'

That was how the most patient instructor in the world found himself running alongside me, clutching the handlebars with his chubby fingers. I learnt how to ride Blue. The problem with Blue was that this was New Zealand and the wind was in my face, and the feeling of freedom was ... was what? It was freezing. I didn't enjoy it. I was scared of the traffic, and I discovered that after all, I was afraid of 'falling off the bike and breaking my back' as my father had speculated. So, no. I was never to ride Blue. Freedom be damned.

I was starting to understand what most of my friends had always known, which was that I saw things in an unconventional way. This often took me to the edge of my crowd of friends.

After the failed biking hobby, I felt an urgent need to connect to my surroundings in this new strange land of the Long White Cloud. I looked for something that would give me and the Engineer purpose while providing the opportunity to meet locals and live outside the expat bubble. One night we read that a local school offered foreign language night courses. English was my home language, but I had studied two other languages at school, and I was not great at either of them.

In fact, one of my teachers insisted that my intelligence was worse than that of a flea. That classroom had fewer seats than children learning, so some of us had to sit around the teacher's desk. After Mrs

Hebrewteacher finished writing on the board that day, she was standing right in front of me, blocking my view of what she had written.

'Sorry, Mrs Hebrewteacher,' I said nervously, 'but I can't see the board. Please could you, like, move a little?'

Mrs Hebrewteacher was always irritated. Her constant shouting could be heard in the corridors. Reason and logic were not always on her side. I once witnessed her hitting a classmate on the head with a Bible for not having the right books.

'If you have a bad viewpoint, move somewhere else,' she snapped.

'Where should I move to?' I looked around the crowded classroom. I couldn't find an easy solution, but she just gave me a blank stare in reply. 'Mrs Hebrewteacher, I don't know where to go,' I persisted. 'Can you, like, step to the side?'

Infuriated, she grabbed me by the sleeve of my dress and pulled me off my chair. I was a very light kid and the force of this propelled me across the classroom where I landed on the floor, utterly humiliated and close to tears. I may have been dumb, bored or flea-brained, but I certainly lost interest in languages that day.

Despite my horrible experience with Mrs Hebrewteacher, the question I asked myself that night in New Zealand was not if I wanted to learn a new language, but which language I should take. While living in Florida, Relationship No1 had spoken Spanish, and it was captivating. I wanted to own that sound. The Engineer wanted to learn French. We flipped a coin, and for the first time in my life, I won.

And so, with the Wellington gale-force winds and sideways rain, we started our first lesson in Spanish. Instead of shouting, Mrs Spanishteacher was encouraging. Instead of beatings on the head, she brought cookies and, most importantly for me, instead of throwing my body across the room, she greeted me with hugs. She entertained us with stories from Latin America and I remembered that I had always wanted to visit that part of the world. I looked up at my man with big green eyes and asked, 'Do you think we can go there one day?'

CHAPTER 4

Around the World

'Take me home with you,' they shouted. Paper dolls of every shape and colour reached towards me from their shelves. Glazed pottery, leather handbags, silver jewellery, vibrant blankets and wooden skeletons called out to me as the aroma of hot empanadas and tacos wafted with the putrid drain water and lively mariachi music. Tourists and locals alike bargained through their day. Little children manned their parents' stalls as fat men sat carving trinkets. In a moment of sensory overload, I reached out and touched a pretty, coloured drinking glass.

'Should I buy this now or when we come back to live here?' I asked the Engineer absent-mindedly as brightly beaded skulls beckoned me with glass eyes.

We were flying home to Wellington the next day, and we didn't have any plans to return to Latin America. We had been to Brazil, Uruguay and Venezuela, but it was Mexico that had bewitched me. I was drawn to the country as if protected by an invisible sarape. I just knew that I belonged in that wild and soft land. As I walked around the artisan markets with the Engineer, neither of us had an inkling of how life changing that Latin

American trip would be.

'Do you remember when we were in the market in Mexico, you asked about buying a glass?' the Engineer asked me two weeks after leaving Latin America. I was in England visiting friends and would be returning home the following week.

'Yes. I still can't imagine why I said that.'

'Well, the office just called to ask me if I would like to go there for a long-term contract. I know how much you loved it there. Are we in or are we out?'

The Engineer and I had been together for about five years. Our thinking was generally aligned and decisions like these were easy for us to make.

At the start of the millennium, we packed up our Kiwi lives and moved to Mexico City just in time to find out that the global fear of Y2K was nothing more than a neurotic tic. I settled down in my newly adopted country, with a residential visa along with the instruction from the government not to find a job. A diminutive Spanish woman named Angeles became my new best friend, and we drove around Mexico City while I absorbed the beauty and variety of this culture. Spanish came quicker than I thought it would, but I found myself craving the sound of English.

'Sabes que? You know what? There is a group of expats who volunteer at an orphanage. Maybe you can to join them,' Angeles suggested as she ran her fingers through her short black hair.

'I don't know, Angeles. I'm not much of a joiner.'

'But this you will like. You help children with the homework. You can ask to work with the three years old or, if you prefer, the five years. I don't think you have enough Spanish for the nine years just yet.'

'Five-year-olds? Three-year-olds? They don't get homework, do they?' I said, even more put off by the idea. I had hated school, and to me the word 'homework' represented torture.

'They learn to read, write and do a little sums at three so they get a little of the homework too.'

'You know me, Angeles. I don't even volunteer to make a cup of coffee, but thanks for thinking of me.'

'The volunteers, they go for coffee afterwards. Then they all speak English.'

'Oh. Well, okay. I'll check it out.'

I felt a mixture of defeat and elation – I could have coffee in English! Suddenly volunteering didn't sound so bad.

CHAPTER 5

Meeting Strangers

'Sorry, it's a bit chaotic today. The younger boys are moving from the boys' building across the road to this side to be with the girls. Unfortunately.'

The volunteer addressing me had a refined American accent. She was a bit older than me, and although she was slight, she possessed a strength I immediately gravitated towards. She had been volunteering at the orphanage for years and was comfortable directing volunteers and workers alike.

Far from the vibrant colours of the tourist area, the orphanage was textured with dingy hallways and sunny gardens. I watched through the doorway as the orphans finished eating while the smell of greasy boiled chicken cut through the pungent smell of sewerage. The grass I was standing on was manicured, but the sandpit was empty. The brightly painted Mexican wall highlighted the half-hearted attempt at kitchen comfort. It felt a bit forlorn to me and I wanted an excuse to leave.

'We'll be up those metal stairs in the homework room,' the American continued. 'Don't be surprised if the kids don't make eye contact – they often don't. No confidence, you know.'

I felt out of place. I looked for something to do with my hands, which suddenly felt too big for my body. I didn't know about kids, let alone mistreated or damaged ones.

'As I was saying earlier, it's much safer for the little ones on this side with the girls,' the woman continued. 'Although ...' Her voice trailed off and I thought I caught a worried expression, but then the door opened and a quiet child came out.

'What's the story with the little boy in smart-man pants?' I asked, feeling inexplicably drawn to him.

'Who? Isaak? You'll be helping his group with their homework.'

There was a colourful kids' poster trying desperately not to fall off the dirty wall as the other children filed out of the kitchen. Hollow laughter emanated from unsmiling faces and I looked back at Isaak. I gave him a nervous smile. He smiled back. There were snotty noses mixed with clean clothes. Dirty faces and fresh looks, all trying to impress the staff and volunteers around them, but my attention was stuck on tidy little Isaak who didn't seem to have the confidence to speak. I watched him pick up one of the other children's pencils and surreptitiously put it in his pocket.

'Okay, we're almost ready,' the American said. 'We're just waiting for Miguel. He's usually last. Be aware that he isn't violent or anything, but he is a very angry child.'

'What does he do? Why is he angry?' I asked.

Her expression was enough to indicate I'd find out for myself soon enough. I didn't have to wait long. Within moments, Miguel arrived wearing a clean white T-shirt and green tracksuit pants. His arms hung loosely by his sides but I noticed his five-year-old knuckles were white as his fingers clenched into fists almost unconsciously. He brought a latent heaviness to the doorway, his small body radiating an inexpressible anger. He took in the scene silently and then sat down with a scowl on his face as though daring me to try to get close to him.

So there I was, with the pencil thief, the angry one and a group of five-year-old kids I was barely ready to assist. I still thought that I was there to selfishly drink coffee and speak English. At a glance, I could see that these forgotten children were accustomed to benevolent people coming and going but they were not well looked after. I gazed at these little children and my heart contracted as I began to realise that their future was about as certain as the picture clinging to the wall.

Growing up in apartheid South Africa, I had seen neglect and indifference in many forms. All too often, black mothers looked after white mothers' children, leaving their own to fend for themselves. Young black children were often expected to earn a living, help sustain the household or even look after aged relatives without seeing their parents for days or weeks at a time. A lucky few were at the centre of their parents' attention, but many were only too aware that they were being overlooked.

At four years old, I realised that Godfrey was my home-friend. While I had plenty of white friends to play with at school, he was the little black child who lived with his mother, Rebecca, in the studio just outside our kitchen. During the day, Godfrey and I would chase lizards around the courtyard and then, after the failed hunt, sit on the hot cement and eat pap with our greedy hands dipping into the same metal pot, listening to kwela music on an old radio. At night, Godfrey was tucked away in his little bed, waiting for Rebecca to finish serving us. I quickly learnt of black people lunches and white people dinners. Not a mix and match, but an unfair separation.

I remember straining to hear the whistle and drumbeat that heralded the arrival of the gumboot dancers in our affluent suburban street. I loved watching those little boys move to the Zulu rhythm they created by stomping the ground and hitting their rubber boots.

My mother, with her fair skin and auburn hair, grew up in a township. It was unusual for white people to live among black people but she was born to immigrants. Like many migrants, her parents had an instinct for survival and did whatever they could to improve the prospects for their children. The township was a pit stop in their lives. As a child, my mother would listen to township music and play with Zulu, Xhosa and Sotho kids. As a mother, she'd often hand us coins to give to these impromptu street performers. Around the world, children the same age were playing games for entertainment, while these black kids of varying ages *were* the entertainment. This was how I first learnt that difference is part of life and that my first-world values shouldn't dictate other people's worth.

Having grown up in South Africa, I thought I understood desperation. But in the orphanage in Mexico, I learnt a new lesson from a different perspective. I soon realised that I was just another newbie who didn't grasp the rules. Just as I was warned to mind my head as I ducked through the doorway, I should have been cautioned to shield my heart too.

CHAPTER 6

Little by Little

The Engineer sat back on our cheap green couch in our rented lounge with marble floors and crystal chandeliers and smiled. 'Anger and pencil stealing aside, they sound cute. Let's volunteer to take them on an outing.' This was after a particularly funny story about the pencil thief finding a box full of pencils and the angry one finding he had none.

I have become used to trying to answer the question, 'Why not have your own children?' Or, 'Why those boys? How did it all happen?' Or even, 'How did you go from being carefree to wanting to be a mother?' I still cannot answer any of those questions easily. I usually tell people that it had something to do with the laws of attraction. I go into raptures of 'just knowing' or even talking about 'love at first date', but the simple truth is I don't know how it happened.

Our first outing started just after breakfast on a Saturday morning. The security guard was accustomed to me arriving on a Thursday to volunteer but he greeted me with the usual Mexican salutation, 'Qué milagro.'

'Hola, poli. This is my boyfriend, the Engineer. We have come to take Miguel and Isaak on an outing for the day.'

As he shook the Engineer's hand, I took some time to steady my nerves. I was worried that the boys wouldn't have a good time, or that one of them would get hurt. I had a number of fears for that day and they all revolved around the boys enjoying themselves. I knew Isaak would be quiet and Miguel would bring his anger along, but I hoped we could give them an entertaining day and provide a peaceful distraction from the usual discord of their weekends.

'Si. Miguel and Isaak, they are waiting,' he said in faulty English.

It didn't take long before we were entering the busy indoor play area of Piccolo Mundo, with its multilevel obstacle courses and coloured bouncy castles. Children from six months to eleven years ran around us. The Engineer and I found ourselves in the midst of the joyous chaos of little boys and girls screaming their tiny, fun-filled lungs out. Instead of being disturbed by the noise and bedlam, we found ourselves joining in. Miguel put down his anger and Isaak came out of his isolation. To the Engineer and I, everything appeared a little brighter that day. We looked around at the sleep-deprived parents slumped in their chairs and we wondered what it would be like to have what they had.

We left at the end of the day, each with a child on a hip and a warm feeling in our open hearts. We dropped a tired Miguel and Isaak off at the home. As we watched them go, carrying leftovers from the food court in their little hands, we knew we would be back the following weekend to take them out again. That night, our house was a little too quiet.

'Did you notice that Miguel was happily chatting to you about the big red slide? He is not usually that engaging. He was just like any other kid there and he didn't even seem to be angry today. You know, I think the outing with us was good for the boys,' I babbled excitedly to the Engineer.

'I know what you mean,' the Engineer said as he munched on some lettuce. 'Based on what you had told me, I expected Isaak to just sit there, but he was laughing and joining in. He didn't talk much, but you could see his smile said everything. And when he came and sat on your lap, the two of you looked so cute together.'

I tried on the word in my mind. *Mom. Mommy. Mum.* For the first time those words had a natural fit for me and I began to picture myself as a mother. I caught a reflection of us in the window and we both had stupid grins on our faces as if we were the first couple to discover the joy of children at play.

The following week, we found ourselves once again talking to the poli and waiting for the two boys to come out. Well dressed and faces cleaned, Miguel and Isaak moved towards us as if we had been doing it for years.

Our outings varied. Movies, or parks or museums. I thought we were bonding. Isaak would come and sit on my lap and wordlessly look up and smile a big smile of what looked to me like contentment. Miguel would run around and come back to us. He was demonstrative, and when we were together I started to think that his anger was receding. I had forgotten that these children were used to outings with visitors. To them, guests were part of a normal life. Strangers were safe because they didn't have time to get close; they came and went. Miguel and Isaak were easily able to block us out as the taxi we had become to them.

At the time, I just didn't understand that the closeness I was seeing was one-sided and that once Miguel and Isaak realised they were bonding with us, the dynamic would change. I did not understand that the smile on Isaak's face was meticulously put there by the persona he had carefully selected just for me to see. I thought he felt what I was feeling. It would be a while still before I began to recognise the mask he instinctively put on for his survival. Similarly, I didn't realise that the reason Miguel did not show us his anger was because to him, the Engineer and I were a moment in time. He felt comfortable only because he knew he wouldn't need to rely on us. He was sure that soon some new stranger would be taking him on outings. I didn't realise that the impenetrable wall that he had constructed would be reinforced the moment he realised he was forming a tie with us. To him, his safety depended on staying foreign. That was how his anger was able to hide in the recesses of his mind.

The Engineer and I thought that our lives were growing together. But in truth, the smiley Isaak was a mask. The happy, anger-less Miguel was only there because *we* didn't matter to *him*. I thought we were good for these little boys, and I will always believe that we were. I just had no idea that the bond I thought we were forming would strengthen only as long as we remained at arm's length and that the promise of loving, caring, trusting people would be the thing that would strain us to breaking point.

'Did you say that the home was going through some changes?' the Engineer asked as we drove towards the orphanage to pick up Miguel and Isaak. We had been making this Saturday trip for a few months now and had fallen into a routine. It was almost taken for granted that we would be picking the boys up on a Saturday morning. This time we were hosting a party for eight kids in the group.

'Yes. The lady who started the orphanage passed away just before I joined. She first started looking after the kids herself. They were never supposed to be adopted out. She wanted to look after them as if they were her kids. Some of them were even given birth certificates with her name on them even though she was too old to give birth. I think it got too big for her to look after on her own and the orphanage became what we know it as today.'

'You mean a place of good intentions and bad outcomes?' The Engineer was always able to sum things up quickly.

'It looks that way. But anyway, I think it is all going to wind-down now. Two kids were adopted out just before I arrived. Not all the people in charge agree with putting the kids up for adoption. Some of them don't like foreigners adopting kids. They think they will be better off in other institutions within Mexico City.'

'As an adoptee, I think family, even a foreign one, is better than an institution.' The Engineer had a close relationship with his mother and I couldn't imagine what would have happened to him if he had been put in an orphanage like the hogar. A lot of our time had become filled with conversations about the boys. We hadn't even noticed that there was a shift; it had just become normal for us to be talking about the boys.

'Don't worry. I'm sure the boys' welfare will be taken into account with all these changes about to happen,' the Engineer said as we turned into the street where the orphanage was.

'Actually, I *am* a bit worried about what will happen to them,' I said. 'I'll ask one of the head volunteers what the next phase will be. There is talk about moving some of the kids to other places, but nothing is certain at the moment.' We had arrived at the gates, and I got out the car and began waving at the poli who was waiting with the boys. These conversations never ended. They were always just put on hold till the next time we could continue them.

One question led to another. And each answer that came our way showed us that these children, to whom we were getting inexplicably close, had no foreseeable future. And they were not safe.

'I spoke to Señora Psychologist,' I told the Engineer while we were preparing our dinner together one night. 'She said that after seven years old, kids don't get adopted out. They either stay there until they can move out on their own or they go to a different institution. It seems like there is no mechanism for adopting a child that age.' I felt bad that we had more food on our table than we would need for two people. I had been at the home earlier in the day and they were preparing chicken soup, but it didn't look like there was much chicken in it.

'How old are the boys again?' the Engineer asked.

'Miguel is turning six really soon and Isaak is a little younger. They are working on all the changes in the orphanage, so I don't think they will be singled out at the moment. There are other kids who are older than them, but I think they are starting to look for other institutions for the teenagers to move to. It is not looking very good for the orphanage in general. In fact, I think they may be closing down.' I had heard differing stories about what was happening to the orphanage and everything was very unclear. 'I have a meeting with the rest of the volunteers tomorrow. We are going to talk about the school holidays. It is basically a given that we'll take the boys as much as possible.'

The Engineer put his arms around me. 'Don't worry, we'll do what we can,' he said with a touch of concern.

I can't say when we finally realised that the questions we were asking were leading down an inevitable path of parenthood. At some point, we must have realised what we were thinking; but in the beginning, our only concern was for our Saturday boys. Our desire to be parents to these boys just grew quietly. We thought less about what we wanted or needed for ourselves. We considered what we could do to help these troubled boys. There was no clear answer, but the more we thought about it, the more their futures looked bleak. We became more aware of the abuses and institutionalisation that was happening in the home. We realised that time was running out for these kids and that there were fewer and fewer opportunities available to them.

We didn't draw up a list of positives or negatives – we simply knew that if we did not help these children, whom we had come to love, they would not have many prospects in their future. We began grasping how much more we could do for our little young friends who had had their innocence shattered way too early in their lives.

In some areas of Mexico, you see children looking after children. They do not get education, food or safety. They become adept at looking after themselves and doing what needs to be done to survive. They are lost to humanity. They grow up with no opportunity and no escape. The next Einstein or Marie Curie could be standing on the street corner begging, with the world missing out on what they might have had to offer. They live on the edge. Scavengers and misfits. We will never know who among these children would have been able to solve concerns about nuclear fission or world hunger because they are not given the chance to thrive.

We wanted Miguel and Isaak to flourish and we feared for their future.

It was not that we sat down one day and said, 'Let's adopt.' We knew we were dealing with damaged kids and that it would not be easy to bring them into a family, but still, we found ourselves researching older adoptions. At the time, the books we came across reinforced our hopes – care, kindness and love would bring them round.

'Señora Psychologist, I wonder if we could see the psychological reports for Miguel and Isaak so that we can fully understand the issues with the boys and how we could best help them. If they need anything, maybe we can provide a bit more for them.'

'Yes, I can give you something next week,' said Señora Psychologist. 'It is good to see people who want to help.'

We waited, but the reports were slow in coming. 'Señora Psychologist, it's been three weeks. Are there maybe problems that you don't want us to know about? Will we get to see any information on Miguel and Isaak at all?'

Señora Psychologist was reassuring. 'Lo que pasa es, what happened is that there is a lot to do so I haven't had time to pull them, but there is no problem. You know that Miguel needs a lot of patience – that is all. You already know that Isaak is a happy but a quiet child and that he sleeps really well. That is a good thing. There may be a few developmental delays but it's normal in an institution. There are no secrets here.'

Still, I couldn't help feel I was missing something and we began to worry even more about these little boys.

Isaak's quiet nature had a depth that spoke to more than just a naturally introverted child. His language skills were below his age group, but then most of the kids there didn't have a strong level of language. There were times that I wondered if it was the words that let him down or if there was a grave problem with his processing. I could see a finely tuned little mind assessing his situation, but he didn't always seem to understand the basics. I felt that things would fall into place when he was safe and not worried about his environment.

Miguel seemed perpetually angry. He would enter a room and even the other volunteers would shiver, anticipating his vexations that were sure to come. It wasn't as if he would have a tantrum. He was not violent. But his determination was indescribable. He would do what he wanted regardless of the situation.

'Miguel, if you have finished playing with toys, they need to be packed away. You know this. Come, I'll help you.' The young Canadian volunteer bent down and started packing the toys into the box. She had already packed all but three away.

'No,' Miguel said. 'I played with them earlier but now someone else is playing with them. They can put them away when they are finished.' Even as we all knew he was fibbing, he walked out the room with the strong conviction that he knew best. In stunned silence, we watched him go.

'I'll go get him,' I said. I was sure that I could coax the helpful boy that I had seen on our Saturday morning outings to come back and complete his chores. I caught up with him on the steps. 'Miguel, I have some pictures of you playing in the park. When you are finished packing the toys away I'll give them to you and you can put them in your album.' I was sure he wanted the pictures and there were only three blocks to put in the box after all.

'I don't need the pictures,' he said as he stood almost eye level with me on the steps. His mood was always churlish at the hogar. I smiled at him and reached for his little waist. I picked him up and swung him around in the air for fun.

'Come on, cariño. Let's go help out,' I said, laughing and setting him down on the ground again.

He stood there and for a minute, the air held its place. Miguel was not laughing. He looked at me with a mixture of rage and disgust. For a split second, I thought he was going to hit me with a closed fist, and for the first time I could see why some of the volunteers were afraid of him.

Without moving a finger or saying a word, he had brought me a feeling of dis-ease and non-violent hostility. In a fog of confusion, I took his little hand in mine.

'Come, let's go look at the pictures. Then we can put away the three blocks and I will help you paste the pictures in the book,' I said as if I hadn't noticed his aggression. Then I led him back to the homework room.

Each week came with the promise but no delivery of the psychological reports that I had requested. I started to wonder if in fact there *were* any reports. Without fully understanding what we were dealing with, we knew there were development issues, deep-seated emotional problems and trauma that the boys had gone through, but the idea of leaving them to fend for themselves became more and more untenable.

We looked at the situation from all angles. We went to speak to an independent therapist to find out what we didn't know about institutionalised children and how best to help them. At the end of the session, all we were confident of was that we could be parents. Making sure the boys were safe became a priority for us. When we asked the questions: who would look after them, who would protect them and who would show them love and comfort, we got no satisfying answers.

Instinctively we wanted to hold up an umbrella of hope to these two boys, the angry one and the pencil thief. We wanted to make their lives easier and so we did our sums. We began to look at how best we could help. We looked at the cost of dentists and doctors, sports activities and good schools. We added up our finances, our emotional resources and any problems we could think of physically, educationally, emotionally and esoterically. There was no right or wrong answer. It was an instinctive choice, not a decision based on a balance of merits. We could help or we could walk away. But it was already too late to walk away. We jumped in with both feet and signed the first letter of interest to adopt.

CHAPTER 7

Yes, You Can – No, You Can't

It was simple. Each time the four of us went on an outing we unlocked more of our hearts. Slowly, we became a bigger 'us'. Each time we signed another form or went to another interview the Engineer and I became more resolved. We didn't look back; we just kept preparing for what was needed next. And a lot was needed.

We were jumping through hoops, proving we were worthy and doing it all in Spanish. Months later we were having meetings with social workers and psychologists, family therapists and caregivers who worked for the department of DIF (the Integral Development of Family) both at our house and at their offices. We had even more meetings with Sara, the lawyer who worked with the orphanage.

'Engineer, what drawing did you do when they asked for a house?' I asked. 'I drew a little house with two storeys and lots of windows,' I continued without waiting for his reply. 'It had a garden path and a big tree with some wooden furniture under it. I tried to draw a bike, but it didn't really look right. The whole thing looked like a child's drawing. I wanted to do so much more but architecture was not part of my training.'

We were on a coffee break and soon we'd need to go back into a grim room to continue the prodding and poking. It felt like they were studying us as if we were aliens, and these were only the pre-home visit trials. Señora Psychologist and Señorita Socialworker had already done the orphanage home study and pre-adoption tests. Now we had to go through the whole thing for the government department.

'I had something similar – I used my engineering drawing techniques. I had me standing on a deck. I also drew a tree. I drew a kiddie swing hanging from one of the branches.'

I knew the Engineer's drawing would look better than mine. After school I had studied fashion design and only knew how to do stylised sketches.

'Aw man, I didn't think to put myself in the drawing. Do you think that's a bad thing? Maybe we should have put kids in the drawing? Or would that have looked contrived?'

'No, maybe putting myself in the drawing says that I am self-centred. Maybe I should have left it out?'

He was mulling it over when the DIF worker called us back in.

'Listo? Ready to answer the forty-page multiple-choice questions now?' she said, as if it was going to be fun.

My head was hurting. Spanish words were mingling with English and the odd Afrikaans word jumping into my confused brain.

Weeks later the knock on our door heralded the dreaded home study. I found it more intrusive than the drawings and three-day question-and-answer sessions we had been through at the DIF office. A kind-looking Mexican lady stood with her clipboard and pen in hand. It was disconcerting to see her expression change from friendly to officious as she put her glasses on her nose. She headed into our kitchen as a place to start. I watched with trepidation as she opened the fridge and picked up the bottle of full-cream milk inside the door. I wondered if I should have bought skimmed milk for this interrogation and my heart started to bang like a bongo drum. Drawers were opened, and books were looked at. I became more concerned with each room we went into as the notes on the clipboard started to cover the pages. With each room we went into, our friendly home studier looked more and more like my enemy. It felt like she stopped short of a full body search – but only just.

Our lives were under a microscope, and everything we said was analysed, scrutinised, probed, dissected and explored.

'How the home study went?' Angeles asked in her less than perfect English.

'Oh, Angeles, I have no idea,' I whined. 'The lady was friendly, but she looked at every single thing and wrote so much down in her book. I spoke to the person who adopted that little girl last year from the orphanage. She said the same thing happened to her. She warned me that, in some overdeveloped, misplaced attempt to protect the kids, they look for any reason *not* to let kids get adopted. They say friendly things and then they write up reports that are damning. I didn't realise how troubling it would feel to have a stranger look at my stuff so carefully. She even looked at a piece of paper I had been doodling on.' I prattled on while making tea. I became aware that with everything going on, I had forgotten to make snacks. 'It felt like they were even judging our colour choices in the house,' I said. 'The room that the kids will sleep in one day is empty and I got the feeling that we should have filled it with toys.'

'They even asked us what time of day we bath. Why would they need to know that?' the Engineer added.

The Engineer and I always pulled together. When other couples found things to fight about, we had a natural way of collaborating. We had a relationship that leaned on each other in times of hardship, and we used humour to get us through. We always felt strong together but it made me uneasy to hear he was worried about the same things I was.

'I have heard it is not easy. All over the world it is the same, no?' Angeles said as she brought a box of pastries out of the packet she was holding. 'Here – I thought you may like these Mexican desserts.' Her caring smile as she put them on a plate made me feel thankful. 'Don't worry. I'm sure they will to see that you guys are the only option for the boys.' Angeles sounded surer than I felt.

'Well, Angeles, it's kinda like we are guilty until proven innocent. They start off by looking for the bad stuff. There is so much abuse happening everywhere so, in a way, it's good that the authorities try to take care of neglected children. There are a lot of bad people who sell children into slavery and worse. I think the laws all started with that in mind.'

'But you are not going to be bad or sell your children. They must to know that, no?' Angeles was saying what I felt but I tried my best to see it from the other perspective.

'Yeah, but they need to make sure about that. The checks are needed, sure. But unfortunately, I think the laws have gone too far in suspecting the worst. I think the children often get overlooked based on that.'

'Is there a problem because you are not Mexican?' Angeles asked gently.

'Um, it could be an extra factor. There are a lot of people who don't think cross-cultural adoption is a good idea. But I don't think they realise how unsafe some of the institutions can be. I think it's better to grow up in a family, any family, than to grow up with the abuses that happen in some of those places.'

Angeles, the Engineer and I stood together in our kitchen, our thoughts muddled.

A lot of people don't realise that the adoption process is so hard. They think if you want to adopt a child, you are welcomed with open arms, but the truth is much more complicated than that. The reasons for the laws are similar no matter what country you adopt from. Some countries are stricter than others, but in most cases, the process is so hard that it acts as a deterrent.

In our case, we were going to have to make sure that these boys were safe and if we were the only people who were interested in their future, then we would go to the ends of the earth to make sure they were okay.

And then it got a little harder.

'Hey, how come you want to adopt? Did you fail at IVF?' one DIF social worker asked me.

This was a question we hadn't anticipated. Until we met Miguel and Isaak and felt that intangible pull towards them, we had actively tried *not* to have a family. When we had sex, we did it for fun, or sometimes to relieve a headache or stress. No temperature checking. No 'Quick, let's do it now while I'm ovulating.' Apart from the idea of a failed IVF attempt, the social workers were also concerned that I might have had a miscarriage or abortion. Two weeks later I found myself sitting in a gynaecologist's office.

'Doctor, if I can't give them proof that I have never been pregnant, DIF won't let me continue with the adoption process.' I watched her face through the blur of my tears. She was elegant, and her shiny black hair lay straight on her shoulders. Her manicured hands passed me a box of tissues. I noticed that she had a small scratch on her arm and I zoned in on that little straight line.

'I am going to help you in any way I can, señora. Lo que passa es, what happens is that the body heals quickly and also sometimes people get pregnant without knowing it. Sometimes the baby doesn't stay, and then there is no sign of that pregnancy either. There is only so much I can say with surety.'

'I'll never be able to have my children.' I felt my heart pumping in my throat. I knew the tears were smudging my eyeliner. I had thought it would be easier.

'There is no test for that. Can you tell me why they need it?'

'I don't know. Someone in their infinite wisdom decided that I need to prove that I didn't throw a child away.' I was trying to regain composure, but I was working myself up instead.

'And the Engineer? Does he need to prove he isn't a father?'

'No,' I wailed. 'He's a man. He could have a hundred babies running around the world.'

The doctor smiled as she leaned forward, touched my arm and then started to write a letter.

With the non-pregnancy test taken care of, we discovered that DIF didn't like us knowing the children we wanted to adopt.

'There are about two million homeless kids,' I told Angeles, 'but they won't let me choose *these* two little boys who have grown in my heart.' I was clutching a picture I had taken of the boys at play, their little serious faces looking directly into the camera. It was far too late for us to turn back now. These boys deserved a family.

'Stupido,' Angeles said. 'These children must to have a family. It is terrible. Are they telling they can be neglected and abused but can't to live with a family who already know them?' Her grammatical errors usually brought a smile to my face, but today nothing could lift my spirits.

It was deeply consoling to share my anger with someone who cared. It had been a shock to discover that, after all, the adoption story I had been living off as a child was a myth.

Apparently, children are not supposed to be chosen.

'What you will do?' Angeles asked.

'I have to go to a therapist to prove I'm not obsessed with these two boys.'

'And the Engineer? Does he also must to go?'

'No. Just me.'

'Stupido,' she said again. 'Everyone can see you four are good together. Doesn't that count? What about they need a home and you have a home for them? Didn't you tell me the orphanage is closing down?'

'Yes, Angeles, yes. The boys would have to go somewhere else, but after they turn seven, they don't get adopted. They will be doomed. All the kids are going to be scattered around Mexico City.' I didn't want to think about what could happen to these boys. They had already lost so much in their lives.

'So, what you will do?'

'I'll do what I need to do,' I said determinedly. 'I'll go to therapy and let them assess and reassess me.'

'Who pays for the session?'

'We do, of course. But, Angeles, these boys need a family. Here, they will have a chance to heal. If they go to another orphanage, who knows what will happen. The older kids in this orphanage didn't do well once they got out. There is only one thing I can do. I need to go prove myself worthy again.'

By this time I had thought I was strong handling the bumps in what was becoming our new life. But it became clear that I would need to be much more skilful when it came to family issues. I didn't know it at the time, but I needed to become battle proficient if I wanted to give my children a childhood. And I was damned if I was not going to give these two children a happy life, even if it came a bit late.

CHAPTER 8

Oliver Guantanamo

Imagine if the orphanage in *Oliver Twist* had an affair with Guantanamo Bay. This orphanage in Mexico City would have been its abandoned offspring. As in many orphanages, the carers were often called Mama. It was some of these misnamed mamas who would stick needles into a child if they wet their bed. It was some of these mamas who would hurt, abuse and steal childhoods from those they were supposed to be protecting. Even the kind ones could not prevent the damage that was being perpetrated. With nobody looking out for the kids, big or small, and with a lack of love and abundance of despair, the inmates themselves became the next line of abusers, turning Oliver into Guantanamo. And who could blame them? They had lessons in their own survival.

People often think that kids in an orphanage long for a family to adopt them, but for the most part, they are wrong. When children have been learning to survive instead of thrive, they can misinterpret their harsh surroundings and learn to trust abuse over kindness. They can grow fearful of compassion. They may even go to extreme measures to keep softness at bay. The tools they use to protect themselves often become weapons of self-destruction. One might try to dismantle their self-imposed 'armaments' by being gentle and loving, but it is not easy to shift a mindset that insists they must never believe they are safe. Sadly, they cannot trust kindness. To institutionalised kids, a kind face feels dangerous. Their field guide is completely different to that of kids who are properly cared for from the time they take their first breath. Fear, abuse and ill-treatment become a deeply rutted track of perpetual misuse marked out for them again and again and again. Like gladiators forced to fight without time to second-guess themselves, some of these children learn that each moment can be perilous and so they live on instinct.

As the orphanage started implementing its closure, one of the volunteers answered a disturbing phone call.

'Señora, I was wondering where I should drop off the meat now that the hogar is closing?'

'Um, the meat?' asked the confused volunteer. She often accompanied the staff to buy meat and they always went to a shop close by.

'Si, señora. And the bread.' The caller spoke more slowly this time.

'But how long have you been delivering?' she asked, becoming increasingly alarmed.

'Años, years, missus.' Horrified, the volunteer asked for the drop-off address. To her dismay, it was not the address of the orphanage. It was the address of one of the people who worked there. She had formed a home industry.

When I first heard the story, I was furious; but after a while I only saw a person living in near-poverty, trying to keep her own family safe. I started to listen more closely and discovered this was not an isolated incident. I heard about a room full of donated clothes that had been rifled through, sorted out and the best picks taken home. The rest of the unwanted clothes were left in the dark, never to be distributed. Toys donated and not received. Toys received and then sold off the day after. The corruption leaked out everywhere.

Some weekends, the adults would leave the orphanage. The older kids oversaw the younger ones. Some of the teenage boys would get the younger boys to fight with each other. They would bet on them like roosters in a cockfight. This became only one of the reasons the small boys were moved to the girls' side of the road. But this didn't improve their safety. The older girls had their own way of making fun.

Years after our sons joined our family, news broke that detainees in Guantanamo Bay had been tortured. Along with the rest of the world, my heart stopped. I was horrified. But what horrified me even more than the reports of torture was being reminded of a similar 'game' some of the older girls in the orphanage had inflicted on the younger kids when there were no adults around: making them stand with their arms held up in mid-air and bending their knees for countless moments. The same method was used against prisoners in GITMO. This torment didn't happen every week. Not all the older kids did this. There were some lovely young people there too. Just not enough.

This orphanage, filled with the best of intentions and the worst of human nature, was the second place where my children learnt about life. Their most formative years were moulded and shaped within its walls, and they would never manage to shake the lessons they had learned in the three years they lived there. At the time, I only hoped to save them from the place. Later in life, I realised that the place had been carved irrevocably into their psyches.

CHAPTER 9
The Duck Plan

The new director had arrived at the orphanage in a whiff of controversy. She was brought in to supervise the closure of the orphanage. La Directora commanded any room she entered – but it was her soft side that won me over. Not wanting Miguel and Isaak to be relocated too many times, she'd arranged for them unofficially to move in with the Engineer and me while the adoption process played itself out. It was at this time that we began to hear a rumour that the older kids in the orphanage had been discussing the adoption of Miguel and Isaak, and that some of the younger kids were talking about it too.

Up until my impromptu meeting about the adoption process with la Directora I had mainly dealt with Señora Psychologist and Señorita Socialworker, who together supervised the children at the hogar. I sat absent-mindedly, twisting my hair between my fingers while she tried to put me at ease. I wished the Engineer was with me. His job was demanding, but his time was flexible. The Engineer and I complemented each other in many ways. His strengths were my weaknesses and mine were his. I always felt that together, we could get through anything.

I chose my Spanish words with care. 'I'm worried that the boys will hear about the adoption in the wrong way,' I explained to her. 'If all the kids are already talking about it, shouldn't we be preparing Miguel and Isaak for the news?' I was trying not to be too pushy, but there didn't seem to be much communication going on.

'I've asked Señora Psychologist and Señorita Socialworker to arrange the transition for Miguel and Isaak. They will need to get used to the idea of coming to live with you guys,' la Directora told me. 'We have a little bit of time but not a lot. They've put together a two-part cunning plan.' She winked at me and began to explain. 'First, los niños will have play therapy with a little duck.'

'What does the duck do?' I asked. 'When will the boys start sleeping over? When will we know that they are ready to make the move?' I had so many urgent questions.

La Directora smiled at me and put up her hands in mock surrender. 'Miguel and Isaak will play with a toy duck who is lonely and needs a family. The duck will speak to different farm animals. One day it will become friends with a cow. After a while, the duck will move into the cowshed. The ducky is loved by the cows, so it doesn't matter that they don't look alike. The boys will have this therapy over the next few weeks. It won't just be one session. The idea needs to slowly grow on them.'

'That's clever,' I said. I felt my body begin to relax.

'Now the second part of the plan. You will continue to have the boys visit on a Saturday or Sunday. Soon we will extend this to both days. When the boys ask to sleep over, we'll slowly extend the nights too until they are ready to stay permanently.'

'Will there be enough time?' I asked, my body reverting to stress mode. The end of the school term was looming and the calendar was in warp drive. 'Once the boys come to live with us, will Señora Psychologist be able to continue to see them? I think it is important for there to be some continuity.' I was trying to make sure that I had thought of everything because I knew the orphanage had not done too many adoptions and it had become clear to me that they didn't have a proper system in place.

'Yes, we can arrange that for you. It is a good idea,' la Directora said, standing up, indicating the meeting was over. 'You can talk to Señorita Socialworker about setting it all up.'

Ominously, in the following weeks, the duck plan didn't transpire. Isaak *did* play with the duck during his play therapy, but it never made it into the cow's house. Miguel never even saw the duck. And the first sleepover came up quicker than we thought it would.

'Señora, I am glad you are still here. It is 5pm and I thought you had already left.' Señorita Socialworker was standing in the doorway of the homework room, watching me pack things up for the day. 'Tomorrow I need you to pick up Miguel and Isaak after school. Can you take them home with you?'

The week before, we had gotten approval to take them out on Saturday as well as Sunday for the first time. I had been wondering how long it would be before we could have a sleepover.

'Sure. Of course. Have they asked to sleep over at our house yet? Or should I just bring them back here for dinner?' I answered excitedly.

'No, no,' she laughed. 'Don't bring them back here. You need to have them for the full weekend. Can you take them to school on Monday?'

'Yes. Yes, of course. How exciting! But are they ready for that? Have they been prepared?' I gushed. I couldn't wait to have a proper weekend with them.

'Well, they haven't been prepared just yet, but it will be fine. Trust me. From now on, there will be no adults staying here on the weekend. All of the little children will be sleeping at volunteers, so it is best that you take your boys.' As Señorita Socialworker started to walk away, I reached for my cell phone to let the Engineer know that we needed to buy beds in the morning.

As a child, I never liked sleeping over at friends' houses. One weekend I had a sleepover at a friend's family farm. It had been raining and the dirt roads were puddle-filled and muddy. We did what kids were expected to do: we went out into the middle of the farm roads and played in the mud.

'You don't know how to do it,' my friend said, laughing as I tried to jump on a dry patch. 'The trick is to find a puddle that has caked over a bit and then gently put a foot on top. Like this. Then slowly step harder.'

I followed her directions and the puddle opened like a pudding with warm chocolate inside. I felt the hot, wet mud oozing between my squelching toes. We returned home very muddy and very content. But when night came, I wanted to go home. The next day my friend's mother did everything she could to make me feel comfortable, but the magic was gone and, finally, she called my mother who made the two-hour trek to their farm to pick me up.

The Engineer and I didn't want the boys to have any nights of quiet discomfort. The boys still had not been told about the adoption and this worried us. But despite the lack of planning, that first weekend was a success. We were careful not to overstimulate them. We wanted the weekend to be as natural as possible. I picked the boys up from school on Friday. The three of us ate lunch and then we did homework together. The Engineer and I had unplugged the TV because we had been warned that the orphanage used it as a nanny and all the children had a bit of a TV dependency. I took the boys into the garden to play. That night as we tucked the boys into bed, the Engineer chose a book and the four of us cozied up to each other while he read.

'Goodnight. Sleep tight. Let the faeries kiss,' I said in English just like my mother had said to me every single night of my childhood.

'Goo ni. Sle ti. Letha fa ki,' they giggled, mimicking me as we turned out the light.

Saturday and Sunday were relaxing days with the four of us playing board games and going to the park. Although the weekend felt natural, we knew that our lives would not be that simple. We understood that Miguel's anger would not simply disappear or that Isaak's quiet way had underlying reasons, but we still believed that love would prevail and that with care and kindness, our sons to be would learn to trust us.

'Eat up, guys. We need to leave for school soon.' I was packing their bags and getting ready to drop the boys off. I felt like a regular mother.

The Engineer smiled at me as he helped the boys with breakfast.

'Can I leave my truck here?' Miguel asked. 'Then he will be ready for me next time.'

'Of course, you can. That's a great idea.' My heart was filled with pride. We'd made it through a weekend and now my soon-to-be child was showing me his approval by leaving his prized truck at our house. The Engineer and I locked eyes, feeling the importance of the moment. Everything looked a little brighter.

But time was running out. A week later, our plans to go slowly disintegrated, just like the duck game had never got started.

'I'm *not* going to visit you this weekend. I am not ever going to visit you again. I don't need to.' Miguel was sitting in the homework room with his arms crossed. Isaak was standing between me and the doorway, trying to decide if he should leave the room or stay to watch the scene unfold. I was perplexed.

'Don't worry, señora, I think he is just scared. I think one of the little ones may have been telling him about the adoption,' Señorita Socialworker explained.

'What? The kids told him? See, this is what I have been worried about,' I said in frustration. I had been trying to get this arranged as smoothly as possible. Now I could feel it blowing up in my face and I could see that my child was the one getting hurt.

'Some of the children are getting restless because they know something is going on with Miguel and Isaak and not them. It is affecting the other children and we have a responsibility to the other kids,' said Señorita Socialworker determinedly. I was finding it hard to swallow my irritation. I hadn't wanted any of the children to be badly affected. That was why I had been asking her to prepare the boys for what was to come. I had been assured that Señorita Socialworker and Señora Psychologist would make every effort to prepare the boys. 'Señora,' she urged, 'we need to move fast now. It will be best for Miguel and Isaak to be living with you by the time school finishes.'

'But isn't it too soon?' I asked.

'You must take them home and then assure them that they will be living with you from now on. There are only two weeks left of school. The sooner they move in with you, the sooner they will settle down. Don't worry. Tomorrow Miguel *will* come home with you,' she said breezily.

I was not as sure about Miguel's compliance as she appeared to be. 'I was told that you were going to prepare them and tell them because it was better to come from the orphanage in a controlled manner. Isn't that what we discussed?' I implored.

There was a reason why the volunteers were afraid of Miguel. At times, his anger was palpable. Because of this, most of the time, he was left to his own devices. He had successfully created a ring of isolation around himself. He was not used to getting attention and that was the way he liked it. He didn't want to like or be liked. That was what made him feel safe. I looked at the scowl on Miguel's face and I could see that this was all going too fast for him. I worried that it would harm his misplaced sense of security.

'We'll make a fun game of it,' said Señorita Socialworker. 'But this weekend you must tell los niños that they are moving into your home permanently. It is too late for the orphanage to tell them now. Now it must come from you.'

The hogar was not doing what it had promised, and we were being left to pick up the pieces of a broken plan.

'We had a good start,' I said, 'but I'm worried that if we rush things, it could backfire irrevocably –'

'I thought you would be happy,' Señorita Socialworker interrupted crossly.

'I *am* happy,' I said. 'I just worry this is going too fast for the boys. You know that both Miguel and Isaak don't like change. Miguel is always angry at life and little Isaak goes around as if he is happy, but the more I get to know him, the more I see that he is using a mask to show people all is fine even though that's not what he's really thinking. The boys have lived here for three years. This is all they know. Any child would be uncomfortable with being taken away from what is familiar to them.

Miguel and Isaak know us, but they don't trust us. The bond has not had time to settle yet. The books tell me that this time needs to be handled slowly so that the child has time to adjust. You can see that Miguel is afraid. That is why he's saying he doesn't want to come visit. It's not that he doesn't like coming to our house – he has a great time when he is there. He is just afraid.'

'Señora, you are overthinking this. The boys will both go home with you tomorrow and you will tell them about the permanence,' she said with finality as she walked away.

Señorita Socialworker was right. Miguel did come home with us after school the next day. We had lunch, did homework and played in the garden; and everything was good. The next day we had a family breakfast, went to the park, played a game and built a miniature townhouse with some wooden blocks. Everything was great. As the day wound down, we cuddled up for the nightly book reading.

Then the Engineer and I took a breath and, with care, confirmed the plan of adoption with the boys. We did our best to hide our nerves, but I think Miguel and Isaak could smell our fear. We were relieved at the acceptance the two boys showed. As the Engineer read the bedtime story, I started to think that the problem I feared had just been in my own mind.

'And we will live here always?' Isaak came back to the topic after the reading. He was wearing a fake smile on his serious face.

'Yes, but you don't have to be scared. We will take care of you and we will love you.' I was starting to learn to read Isaak. I understood that he kept people at bay in a different way to Miguel. I had begun to understand that his smile was a mask and that he was not as happy as he pretended to be. An independent psychologist had warned us to keep an eye on this, in case it indicated underlying issues of attachment or even possible depression.

'I want to watch TV now,' was all Miguel said, changing the subject abruptly.

'Miguel, I know this is a big change. Do you want to talk about it?' I was following a guideline I had read.

'TV,' he said as he sat up and crossed his arms, clenching and unclenching those little fists. 'I don't want to go to sleep here. I'm going back now.' Miguel's voice was suddenly stony cold and determined. And at that point, everything fell apart. He began hitting the wall. He was shouting incoherently, at us and to us. He'd had a nice day but it was now being ruined by the realisation that he was starting to feel loved. He had been given attention and was not comfortable. We tried to reassure him, but he was beyond reason.

'Let's try to call the orphanage,' the Engineer said. 'Maybe he can talk to Señorita Socialworker and she can assure him that it will be okay.'

'I already tried. There is no one there. All the adults have left for the weekend and only the older kids are there with the poli. I tried all the numbers I have but I don't have anyone's home number.'

Miguel was still in attack mode, reminding us why the volunteers were afraid of his six-year-old adult anger. 'I don't need to sleep here if I don't want and you can't make me.' He pointed at Isaak. 'And you can't make him either.' His little face was red; his fists were tight.

I didn't want to force him. But none of us had any choice. While the Engineer tried to console Miguel and Isaak, I phoned Angeles in tears. 'I need to tell the boys that we will love them and look after them and keep them safe, but my Spanish is lost.' The words tumbled out my mouth in a disjointed muddle. I felt as though our boys were moving beyond our reach.

'You must to calm down,' Angeles said. 'Tell me and I will tell you.' Her gentle voice brought me back to the moment. I explained our story and she told me how to say what I wanted to say. 'Come, we practise together.'

When I went back into the room, the Engineer had managed to calm Miguel down, and he was sitting with Isaak on his lap and Miguel in front of him. He was reading another story and I could see his eyes were red. I sat next to him and waited for the story to end before I launched into my prepared words.

Miguel was still angry, but he had calmed himself down. 'In the hogar, we are allowed to watch TV. I am not going to sleep till I can watch some TV.' We realised that Miguel needed to feel a small degree of control.

It had already been a long night. As the four of us lay as close to each other as was comfortable, we watched a little bit of TV. That night we all fell asleep with tears in our eyes. The next morning I managed to get hold of la Directora, and she spoke to Miguel and Isaak over the phone. For the rest of the day I trod as carefully as I could. I felt a flaw had been rendered into our fabric and I hoped we could mend it. The day went smoothly but I couldn't help wondering if we had turned a corner or if we were only just about to reach the precipice.

On Monday morning, as we packed up, I noticed Miguel watch my reaction as he deliberately gathered up all his things.

'Miguel, you can leave the truck here if you want,' I said, my voice and chest tight with apprehension.

'I don't want to. The truck is mine. He will come with me.' With careful deliberation, he put the toy truck in his bag. Evidently, the duck was going home, and he would not be tricked into the cowshed again.

After dropping the boys off at school, I was summoned to Señora Psychologist's office. 'I hear you had quite a weekend with Miguel. How did Isaak seem?'

'He had a fake happy look on his face the whole weekend,' I said. 'I think things are going too fast for them.'

'Hmm. How are *you*?'

I wanted to shake her heavyset shoulders, but instead I watched her unhurriedly tidy her desk.

Finally, as she pulled her chair out and sat down heavily, she took pity on me. 'Señora, this week must be their last at the orphanage.'

'That's way too fast,' I protested. 'This weekend showed it. The little ones can't handle going so fast.'

I realised that school holidays started in less than two weeks and then the orphanage would dissolve. The Engineer and I could handle anything that was to come, but instinctively, I knew that these diminutive people could not cope with this neck-breaking speed. Their way of life might not be a healthy one, but it had been their reality for three years. In between torture and abuse, they had friends to lean on. Now they were going to live in a big house with people they had not yet learnt to trust. But at this point, no argument the Engineer and I could make could slow the process down.

CHAPTER 10
Unfamiliar Road Home

'No quiero una mama.' I don't want a mama. Miguel looked up at me with his big brown six-year-old eyes. I held on to his little sleeves, knowing that he did not like the feeling of touch on his skin. I wished I could hug him.

'I don't need to be your mama. I'll just be your very good friend.' Holding back tears, my voice sounded strangled and unfamiliar to me. I reminded myself how I had reached this point. How I'd started helping at the orphanage because I wanted to hear the infrequently used language of my childhood while partaking in the cake and coffee at the shift's end. Now I was not wanted. Told I was not needed. As an outsider, I did not belong. To soften the blow, I told myself that this child was telling me to take it slow.

So I stood in the dark office, holding my breath as I waited for Miguel's response to my assurances. La Directora stood behind us. She held her breath too.

Earlier, I had arrived to find that Miguel and Isaak's departure from the orphanage had been given to Carlos to manage, despite him having terrible flu that day. Carlos was in his late twenties, studying to be a priest when he first arrived at the orphanage. By the time I had started volunteering, he had been there for over two years and his life had taken a tangent. Soft-hearted Carlos was one of the few workers who took an interest in the children and they looked to him for direction.

Carlos's instructions from Señorita Socialworker were clear, so he and I reluctantly attempted to follow her script. It set a scene of a fun-filled goodbye, with the boys hopping into my green Golf Polo and our newly formed family driving off into the polluted sunset. He had also been given a plan B – a plan I wasn't aware of.

I waited patiently for Carlos to get out of his sick bed. When he finally emerged, he looked like a puffed-up blue Michelin man. Swaddled in three jackets, his head was wrapped in scarves and cotton wool poked out of his ears. The kids ran around making fun of him and started saying goodbye to Isaak, but Miguel refused to get into the car. Carlos had no choice but to implement plan B.

That day I discovered the trick to piling eight kids and two adults into a two-door, five-seater car. Confused and worried about seat belts, I drove, as instructed by Carlos, to a nearby house. The family there had a fluffy Maltese poodle and it had been Señorita Socialworker's idea that playing with the dog would relax Miguel. When we got there, Carlos stayed in the car, so Miguel stayed in the car. There was no tricking him. The other boys and girls spent a few minutes playing with the dog, then piled back into the car. I started to drive off. When I reached the corner, Carlos suddenly jumped out of the car, telling all of the kids to get out too. As Miguel and Isaak were about to jump out with the others, Carlos closed the door and shouted at me, 'DRIVE, DRIVE, DRIVE,' and I took off in a confused panic. As I looked in the rear-view mirror, I saw Carlos standing in the road, wiping tears from his face.

Miguel started screaming, 'CAAAARLOOOOOSSSSS, CAAAARLOOOOOSSSSS.'

There was no way I was going to take Miguel home with me this way. With Miguel still screaming, Isaak sitting with his alert button set to 'on' and tears streaming down my own face, I drove to the corner shop.

'Miguel, stop crying, querido. We are only stopping to get sweets for everybody. Then we will go back to your friends. Come, let's go choose some sweets.' I was still crying when I called the Engineer. 'If I take him home now, he will think Carlos abandoned him and that I stole him away. We can't go home like this. I trusted that Señorita Socialworker knew best but this is the worst possible way to do this.'

'I'll call la Directora and let her know what's going on,' the Engineer said.

'She isn't there. And I don't think she would have approved this.'

'I'll track her down and ask her to go to the home and meet you there. She is good with Miguel. She will work something out.' He sounded confident.

By the time I got back to the orphanage, la Directora was waiting at the gate. She took Miguel by the hand and led him into her office. They talked for a long time while I sat on a bench wringing my hands. When they came out, Miguel looked directly at me and uttered those fateful words: 'I don't want a mama.' Knowing that the children referred to the cold-hearted carers as 'Mama', I suddenly understood what Miguel was saying. My heartstrings snapped for the first time with that one innocent sentence. I would have to come to terms with the idea that for our children, words like love, trust, security, family, mama, and daddy did not connote safety. Instead, they meant fear. A simple 'I love you' was not an effective way to put a child to sleep. A humble 'You're safe' did not comfort them. A modest 'We're all family' did not have the grounding it should have. These were words and concepts that had been tried and rejected.

I waited for Miguel's response. None came. I saw the determination in his face and noted the little hands balled into fists at his sides.

'I don't need to be your mama,' I repeated. 'I'll just be your very good friend.'

Nothing.

'I tell you what. Let's just give it a try,' I said as a last hope.

Miguel said nothing. He just turned and walked away.

CHAPTER 11

The Broken Promise

While Miguel didn't want to leave the orphanage, Isaak was the opposite, making me promise that I wouldn't force him to go back in the weeks that it remained open. His instinct was to get out and stay out. Like a hunted animal, he was constantly gauging his parameters to improve his situation. He was not being manipulative; it was a matter of survival. He could be cute, funny, smart, aloof or intense as needed, with an uncanny ability to modify his appearance without so much as a change of clothes. Like a social scientist, he instinctively knew your expectations of him even before you did. I would watch this little guy work a room like a professional infiltrator.

'You know, once when Isaak was still in the orphanage, I took him to McDonald's,' Maria, a volunteer, told me as we watched Miguel and Isaak playing in my garden. Maria had managed to sneak out of Cuba when she was in her twenties. These days she lived a life of elegance, but she too had known hardship. I wanted the boys to know that the volunteers who had looked after them in the orphanage could still be a part of their lives, so I made a point of inviting them to our house as often as I could. I recognised continuity was important.

'When I take him out, he usually doesn't finish his food,' I interrupted. 'He liked to take it back to the orphanage with him. Even if he was hungry, he would still keep some back.' I was waiting for her to tell me that all children did that, but she didn't. She simply smiled and carried on with her story.

'He finished his chips and then asked me for more. I told him to first eat his burger. But no, he did not want to eat it. He'd spied a family sitting next to us. Right before my very eyes, he changed. His head hunched into his shoulders. He looked dishevelled and sad. I don't know how he did it, but he even looked a bit dirty as he turned towards the family. He had a far-off look on his little face and in the smallest voice he said, "Please, just one chip. One chip is all I really need." I'm telling you, it was a different child sitting before me.'

'What happened?' I laughed, but I was also aware that the story ran deeper than a request for chips.

Maria grimaced. 'They gave him all their chips,' she said, 'and then they gave me a harsh look.'

The children in the orphanage were never grubby and they were always overdressed. Even on hot summer days, Miguel and Isaak would wear thick undershirts, T-shirt, dress shirt and often a sweater. They always wore socks and shoes and long pants. The Engineer and I had to teach them to wear a T-shirt and shorts with sandals on warm days. Most importantly, we had to teach them that it was acceptable to be dirty.

In those early days, I'd take them into the garden and plant flowers with them. I would get myself excessively muddy so that they'd understand it was okay to lose oneself in fun. It was months before they could learn the joys of mud cakes and wet soil sloshing around their feet. Our little family experienced some things in reverse: at times, it was the parents begging the children to be children, and it was the children who struggled to understand this type of innocent freedom. Quintessential childishness did not come naturally to our boys.

As a child, my mother and I used to have tea parties with my dolls.

We would sit at the little table and drink pretend tea and eat pretend cakes as we offered the toys more of everything. On hot days, she would take the garden hose and spray the water in an arc, encouraging me to run through the cold mist, clothes and all, revelling in the fun. This was the entertaining part of being a child, and I felt sorry for anyone who was deemed too old to take part in the game.

One particularly hot Mexican day, I impulsively grabbed the hosepipe and aimed it at Isaak. The spray soaked him to the core. The look of shock and delight on his face was comical.

'Otra ves. Again, again,' he excitedly yelped as he stood amongst the newly planted flowers, sopping wet. Miguel stood next to me, enjoying the spectacle until it was his turn.

Unfortunately, he didn't think it was as humorous when he was at the mercy of the hose. He read it as an act of aggression and returned the favour by shouting at me as if I was the child and he the adult. Then he stormed off as Isaak and I laughed.

To say that that none of us was ready when the boys moved in is an understatement. Miguel was not comfortable with change. He did not trust that kindness would do him any good and he had been taught by life that he should not rely on anyone but himself. The only way I could make sense of this was to imagine that every time he had let someone get close to him, they had harmed him. It was the only explanation I could come up with for his reactions. His neuropathways had learned their lessons in the most complete way. He did not want to become part of a tribe or group or family. He wanted to be left alone.

Isaak hid behind a disconcertingly permanent fake smile. At the time, I had thought he was a happy, yet quiet child, but as I got to know him better, I started to understand who he was behind his fears. Not having had care in his formative months of life, he had not learnt how to love. For his protection, he had learnt to survive and that meant he needed people to think he was cute. And so he would be cute or funny or quiet. He would be anything you wanted him to be. He just didn't know who or what *he* wanted to be.

The truth is, even if there had been no rush, we would never have been able to fully prepare for the onslaught of becoming adoptive parents. The usual daunting parental matters worried us, but while my friends were focused on their children's future, I had to fathom my children's past. At that stage, I had never heard of attachment disorder, but I didn't need to know the words to understand that our children could not trust that something good might happen to them. So much had happened in their short, dramatic lives and they'd become accustomed to challenging situations. Neither of them had ever received a lesson in kindness.

I was less worried about Isaak because I hadn't fully understood the implications of his fake happiness. At the time, it felt like a more pressing challenge for Miguel to accept that becoming a family was not only inevitable, but also a good thing for him. I came up with a plan to help him embrace his new future. I drew up a contract for each day with some little drawings, sketching the week's arrangements. Everything was illustrated: brushing teeth, eating, dressing, outings and downtime.

'Miguel, while the orphanage is still open, you have the choice to sleep there three nights during the week and visit four days of the week,' I told him.

'I don't want to go there,' Isaak interrupted. 'You said I wouldn't have to.' At every turn, Isaak reminded me of my promise.

'You don't have to,' I told Isaak, 'but Miguel wants to visit. So we'll drop him off at the hogar and then, because you are not comfortable going back there, you and I will do something on our own. You won't have to go in, but we will have to drop him off.'

'What if you change your mind? Will I have to sleep here all the nights?' Miguel said; his eyes narrowed in suspicion.

'Miguel, I've already agreed that I can't change things but if you choose to, you can decide not to sleep there or visit in the daytime. You must sleep here four nights in the week though.'

'Who will decide what we are going to do?' he asked, still unconvinced.

'We all will. Tonight we are going to make a fire and toast

marshmallows. We already have a whole lot of ideas. We just need to decide when to do what. That is what you and Isaak will help me plan.'

'Are we still going to get the luminous stars for the ceiling of our room?' Isaak asked. He was very keen to go to the toyshop and show me some of his favourite toys.

'Yes.'

'And you said we could go to the school-holiday activities every day.'

'Yes, Isaak, you will go every day, but Miguel may choose to go to the orphanage some of those days.'

'What if I want to go to the home all the time?' Miguel asked.

'Miguel, you can either go there in the day or sleep there at night. Up to four days and up to three nights, so you'll be able to see your friends most days or nights.'

'What if – '

'Mi corazón, let's just give this a try. Shall we get started?' My head was saying this could work, but my heart was afraid that it wouldn't.

We finished the 'binding agreement' and signed our names on the dotted line. Me with a firm and practised pen and the two little boys with shaky yet determined hands. As I put the pen down, it occurred to me how much my life had become ruled by contracts and negotiations.

'I'll pick you up after breakfast,' I told Miguel. 'We'll need to leave a bit early because the camp is further from the orphanage than it is from here.' I was about to pack his bag so he could sleep at the orphanage.

He thought for a minute, weighing up his options, and then he surprised me. 'I'll sleep here tonight. It will be a problem if you have to come pick me up.' He walked determinedly out the room, leaving the empty bag between me and the door. I sat there for a few minutes as it dawned on me that he needed an excuse to stay. The second night he was supposed to sleep at the orphanage, we had just finished putting the stars on the boys' bedroom ceiling.

'Miguel, we had better start packing your bag,' I said. 'It's getting late. I need to drop you off before dinner.'

'I think I will sleep here tonight so that I can see the stars shine,' he said.

'That's a lovely idea. But the stars will shine every night so if you want to sleep there tonight, they'll still be here tomorrow.'

'No,' he said. 'I want to see the stars for the first time with Isaak.'

The Engineer and I absorbed each little win as we watched Miguel gradually move into our space, our house and our lives.

The next day was an orphanage day for Miguel and he was looking forward to seeing his friends. Señorita Socialworker confirmed the drop-off time. She would take the kids to the park when Miguel arrived. The closer to the orphanage we got, the quieter Isaak became. The quieter Isaak got, the chattier Miguel became. He could not wait to tell his friends about the sparkly ceiling that he had made 'on his own'.

When we arrived at the orphanage, I immediately knew something was wrong. There was none of the general high-pitched screeching that usually came from three-year-old Juan. Juan didn't have too many words to choose from. He would stand in front of the poli and just emit a yell, indicating that he wanted to engage with him. I didn't see Fanny's big brown eyes peering through the hole in the gate as usual either, and there was none of the usual clanging from the workers behind the wall. I scanned the street for the big red van that drove the kids around but it was not parked outside where it usually was.

The poli came out to greet us. 'Hola, que milagro.' He looked worried. 'There is no one here.'

'But I just spoke to the señorita. I told her we were on our way.' I could hear the panic in my voice.

'Sorry, señora, but they left. You can come in and phone if you want.'

We had been doing so well. I was afraid Miguel wouldn't understand that this was not my fault. With my emotions hanging on a thread and my heart pumping so hard I thought it would burst from my body, I turned to the boys and said, 'I can fix this. All we need is to go inside so that I can call them.'

And that was where it all fell apart. Miguel started screaming at me. He didn't want to wait another minute. He wanted his friends there *now*.

Isaak started screaming that he did not want to go inside. I had a child on either side of me, one pushing towards the gate and the other tugging me back to the car. At the exact same time, they both yelled in disgust and accusation, 'You *promised* me!'

I had promised them. I had promised Isaak that he would never have to set foot in that place again and I had promised Miguel that he would go back for the day. In one fell swoop, I had broken my promise to both of them.

CHAPTER 12

Feelings

Gradually, we found a routine with morning school runs, afternoon playtime, evening dinners and bedtime reading. What we did was no different to any other family but our challenges were intertwined with the mundane. While other children were indulging in sibling rivalry and bedtime rebellions or tantrums over who would sit next to Mum, we were trying to get to know our children and desperately attempting to show them that love was all they needed. What I needed was a crash course in child psychology.

'Miguel, what is the little bear feeling? Can you choose a face to put on his body today?'

We were sitting in front of the soft headless bear. His faces were in the felt pockets sewn into the mat besides his puffed-up body. This toy was developed to show toddlers the words used for emotions. When I saw it in the shop, I knew it would become part of our homemade play therapy.

Once again, Miguel placed the angry face on the bear. 'Today he is angry,' he said.

'He was angry yesterday too. Do you think we can cheer him up today?' I asked.

'I don't know,' Miguel said. Then he walked away, bored with the game.

'What about you, Isaak? What face do you think the bear should have today?' I asked, already guessing what he would choose.

'He is happy,' Isaak said so as not to disappoint. Isaak's own face did not show me happiness even though he had a smile on it. His eyes were sad but he and the bear were always happy.

I'd observed that Isaak could not maintain eye contact, but he was always smiling, and in those early days he never got upset. If he was left alone, he was content to remain in one spot and play; but when people were near, he always joked around. He'd sit on all my friends' laps, playing with their hair. They all commented on how loveable he was. It took some time for me to realise just how much of this was an act. When he was with someone, they appeared to be the most important person in the world to him. That was until he was with the next person. Everybody, anybody, *nobody* was who he would attach to. He would *pretend* to be happy because he didn't know other emotions existed. He didn't know if he was happy or sad because he didn't understand what emotion was. Emotion was a useful mask, not a feeling. He would position himself in the room so that he could always run out, and he would position himself in a relationship that way too.

I tried everything I could think of to help him. 'Isaak, come sit on my lap and tell me how old you are feeling today,' I would often say.

'Three,' he'd say, holding up his fingers.

I'd sit with him cuddled up in my arms as best as his six-year-old body could fit while I rocked him and touched his nose and face as if he was a baby. 'Chi-qui-ti-to,' I would sing in a high-pitched voice, 'li-tt-le one, don't be scared.' I'd rock our bodies and sing a baby song I'd made up just for him.

'Now I am four,' he'd say, this time showing me four fingers, and I'd sing the same song in a deeper voice. Rocking less and holding him as if he was a toddler sitting on my lap. This would go on until we reached the age of nine, by which time he'd be sitting next to me. I had started playing this game on instinct because sometimes Isaak acted like a three-year-old and, at other times, his abilities were closer to those of a nine-year-old. He was not one or the other age, he was all of them. It made it a challenge understanding which age group he fell into at any moment.

The school holiday programme had begun, and I was thankful that it gave all of us a little break from the intensity of our new situation.

'I called you in to see how things are going. Are the boys fitting in well?' The headmistress of the Montessori school asked as the Engineer and I walked into her sunny office. When it came to the boys, he and I did as much as we could together. The sound of children at play made me smile.

'Well, the school is great,' the Engineer told her. 'We're experiencing a few bumps at home as we get to know our children better, but that's to be expected. Our paediatrician recommended we do a few health checks for the boys. He suggested some blood tests and a brain scan so that we have a base level for our sons.'

'Actually, that is a good idea,' said the headmistress. 'I wanted to suggest a psychologist.'

'I had arranged for the orphanage psychologist to continue seeing the boys, but she came to one appointment and cancelled the rest. We've started talking to a family therapist now. Are there any issues you are having with the boys?' I asked with worry creeping into my voice.

'Well, no. Not really,' she said. 'There are a few developmental things we have noticed but I think those will even out with time now that they're in a family. I've been thinking it would be a good idea for the boys to have speech and linguistic therapy. It'll help Miguel catch up his language skills. Isaak might have a few processing issues and the linguistics might give him a boost too.' She smiled reassuringly. 'It's normal for institutionalised children to be behind, so don't worry.'

'Yes, we've noticed they still speak like toddlers,' the Engineer told her. 'It's because they didn't get much adult contact and stimulation in the orphanage.'

The headmistress had a PhD in child psychology and I trusted her advice. 'I would like to suggest a psycho-pedagogic test to see where they are at,' she said. 'Because no one knows much about your kids, this will give us information in case there are any issues. Depending on what is needed, there are some things the school can provide if there are learning or processing disorders.' She reached over and gave my hand a little squeeze. 'Are there any other things we needed to discuss?'

'There is a little thing,' I said a bit shyly. 'They call us by our first names. They aren't comfortable with anything else, so for now, could you let the teachers know not to correct them if it comes up?'

The Engineer dropped the boys at school each day on his way to work while I spent the morning doing chores, researching adoption of older children and preparing for the unending adoption process. My Spanish lessons had come to an end and, ironically, my days were now filled mainly with Spanish. By the time I had to pick the boys up from school, my head hurt from all the morning appointments. The boys and I would do homework together and then, as much as possible, I tried to play with our new sons.

Between speech therapy, family therapy and the rest of the adoption process, the days went by very fast. Our situation was vastly different to what most therapists were accustomed to, and we found that we were often forced to deal with our family challenges with knee-jerk reactions and gut feelings. In many instances, I was sure my gut didn't know what it was talking about. With resolve, the Engineer and I made it through the days while the boys followed suit with their chaotic form of anger and fake happy solitude. The adoption process wound on relentlessly.

In the past, whenever Miguel had let anyone get close to him, they had neglected him. In short, he'd learned to rely on himself alone. Unlike smiley Isaak, Miguel hardly ever smiled. He rejected every effort we made to comfort him when he was upset. His defiance was often confusing.

'Now we must get burgers,' Miguel demanded as we came out of the dark cinema one day.

'Remember we are going to eat at home,' I said. 'I have your favourite burgers ready.' I was not expecting a problem because this arrangement was in our daily contract.

'No. We need to eat a burger now,' Miguel demanded.

'That is what we have at home,' I reminded him.

'No. We must eat here. I am not leaving,' he said defiantly.

'Okay, Miguel, if you are that hungry, this time we can eat here,' I said, making the first mistake of parenting by giving in to his demands too soon. Isaak stood next to me, disinterestedly smiling at the lady standing next to him.

'*Nooo*, we can't eat here!' Miguel shouted with all his might.

I'd expected him to give up the fight after getting his way, or maybe to push the boundary by demanding ice cream, but my child was shouting at me because I'd said he could have what he wanted.

'Miguel, you are confusing me. We have burgers waiting at home, but you said you wanted to eat here. Now I am saying we can eat here and you are shouting at me. What is it that you want?'

'I want to eat a burger, but you said we must go home,' he said as if that made it clear to me.

'Then there is no problem. We will have burgers,' I said calmly. 'The question is where do you want to eat them – here or at home? You tell me.'

'No. We can't.'

'Can't what?'

'We can't.'

That was all he said, with his feet planted on the floor. He didn't move one way or the other. Knowing that he still didn't like the feeling of touch, I was careful not to have skin on skin as I picked him up and walked towards the parking lot while he continued to yell in my ear. Once again, we'd been having fun at the movies and then the argument ensued. I didn't realise at the time that it wasn't about where we ate or what we ate. What Miguel thought he needed most was to keep me at a distance by having an argument.

For no clear reason, each day the tension ratcheted up a bit more until one day I came into the boys' bedroom and Isaak and Miguel were having a disagreement. As I walked in, Miguel lunged his tiny hands towards Isaak's leg and he squeezed it as hard as he could. It was the last straw for me. I had been patient and it wasn't working.

'Stop that right now!' I shouted. 'Why are you hurting Isaak's leg like that? I have had it with you bossing everyone around!' My face showed my anger as I stood there yelling like a banshee. The boys both stood there for a moment in surprise. 'Now get ready. We are all going to the shops,' I said, storming out the room, trying to gain composure.

Surprised at hearing my raised voice, the Engineer appeared. 'What just happened?' he asked.

'I just lost my temper. I don't know what happened,' I said, feeling humiliated.

Nobody said a word until we were all ready to leave the house and then, as if it was the most natural thing in the world, Miguel took my hand and walked out to the car with me. Submissive, compliant, obedient. Hand in hand. Skin on skin. I began to accept that my child required an authoritarian and I was beginning to think that against my nature, I would need to learn to become one.

I was constantly looking for ideas to help my children settle into our family life. One day when the boys were at school, I walked past a veterinary clinic in Las Palmas. A big sign announced that they were selling my dog. It wasn't actually my dog; it was the one I hoped to own one day. A Rhodesian Ridgeback. I *had* to investigate. Just beneath the poster, a disinterested cat sat in a box with her tiny offspring. As I bent down to look at them, the vet came out. 'You want los gatitos?' he asked, pointing at the kittens, who were desperately trying to get to their mother's teats.

'Not really.'

'The mother – she bad. No like the children. They starve. She no care.'

'I just stopped to look at the sign about the dog,' I explained.

'Los gatitos – free.' He turned to go inside and started smiling as he saw me take my phone out of my pocket.

'Hey, don't you think we should get a pet for the boys?' I asked the

Engineer, the sound of meowing in the background. 'I just came upon some kittens.'

'But I'm allergic to cats,' the Engineer said.

'Really? I didn't know that.' Silence. 'They are so cute.'

The meowing continued beside me as I waited for a positive response.

He took a deep breath and sighed. 'Well, okay. I can see you have your heart set. Maybe I'll get used to it.'

The Engineer was always ready to support me and the boys, and I felt a little bit guilty as I walked away with a soft kitty in my hands.

We spoke to the boys in Spanish, but it didn't matter which language we used. The Engineer and I had to accept that showing our children love and kindness did not help them to feel safe. I realised that I would need to find a unique way of teaching the boys what home meant.

In the hopes that the boys would empathise with the kitten, our beautiful Cazadora became an effective tool to communicate with them. Everything that was hard for our scared, disorientated children to hear became the thing they told the kitten.

'Guys, she is scared. She doesn't know that she will be safe with us. Let's show her that she doesn't have to worry,' I said.

'We are going to make sure you are always safe. We already love you so much,' Isaak told her.

'I know you have been through a tough time. Don't be scared. You are living in a new house with a new family and we will look after you,' Miguel said as he hugged her trembling little body.

'We will always love and look after you,' they declared with very serious faces.

Soon, in this DIY therapy, our boys echoed all the sentiments we were trying to teach them. I can't say our daily routines became peaceful, but at some point, we fell into a pattern. With each day, no matter how hard it was, I was thankful that our soon-to-be children were safely with us and not at the orphanage.

CHAPTER 13

The Powers That Be

'Angeles, we got the latest home-study report back from the DIF.'

I was feeling a little dejected. The official report had gone directly to the orphanage and it was the orphanage that gave us a copy.

'I want to hear all,' said Angeles. She knew about all the meetings, which were in Spanish, and sometimes she helped me prepare for them.

'They tell me that I always avoid conflict, but then later in the report they say I am aggressive and look for conflict. Then the report says that I would be too soft as a parent and again later, it says I would be too unyielding. In one part of the report, they refer to a comment I made about my parents who supported me when I was young, and when I was ready to become an adult, they helped me with that as well. In the first part of the report, they talk about this as a good thing but later they refer to it as a bad thing, saying that my parents just left me to become an adult. I don't understand.'

Angeles sipped her tea and thought about it for a moment. 'Wait, that one is complicated. Which Spanish word you used for support? Maybe you use the word that means weighing down instead of holding up. What else did they say? Come, we go through it all and see what we do.'

'They say that I'm too harsh, too soft, too demanding, not demanding enough, healthy, unhealthy, interested and uninterested.' I took a breath but then dove right back in before Angeles could add anything. 'And you know our TV room has all those pretty cushions on the floor?'

Angeles burst out laughing. 'Yes, I remember when you had them made. You asked the sales lady if they made testicles instead of cushions. When she asked what type of testicles you wanted, you said, "Big ones. Gigantic ones. To the floor." I remember how she politely said that they would be happy to make the testicles for you. She used the word you used so that you wouldn't feel silly.'

I laughed at the memory. The shop was an elegant fabric boutique with an immaculately dressed assistant to match the setting. Her lips had hardly twitched, but her smiling eyes hinted that I had made a mistake. It felt like a lifetime ago.

'Well, they wrote in the report that the phone in that room is on the floor. Can you believe it?'

'Well, you know, at least that one is true. Your phone *is* on the floor.' We laughed again.

'What does the report say about the Engineer?'

'It's all the same. It says he is too patient and too impatient, too soft, hard, demanding, not demanding enough, too giving, not giving enough, too logical, too illogical – and of course, the phone is on the floor.'

'It will be okay, no?' Angeles asked me, and this time I heard a little anxiety in her voice.

'No, Angeles. Because of these confusions, the report says that we may not be able to adopt the boys. Remember what I was told they look for any reason to say no to adoption? With the conflicting report from the DIF, it is not looking good.' Our laughter stopped dead.

'What you do now?'

'Now? We can't walk away now. We've been living together for months. Growing and changing to instil some normalcy into these boys' lives. It's not smooth, but they are safer now than they have ever been. They have more opportunities than they've ever had. You know that once a kid turns seven they won't get adopted. What will happen to them?'

I had started pacing up and down the room. My voice had become shriller with each sentence and the room, which was usually bright, seemed to darken. My tea tasted bitter and the cake too sweet.

'And so, what you do now?' Angeles asked, her forehead wrinkled in concern.

'We spoke to la Directora. She is going to see if she can arrange an English home study. She is worried about cultural misunderstandings.'

'Good idea. Who knows how many times you said testicles.'

We returned to meetings that lasted entire days. This time in English. Finally, we were deemed eligible, but it didn't mean that the process was over. Much like a Brothers Grimm story, it would be months before we were called before the judge and even more time would pass before our adoption lawyer, whom we referred to as Sara la Mala – Sara the Bad – showed us just how indifferent she could be.

At the beginning of the process, Sara's black cropped hair and blue eyes gave us hope at each meeting. She seemed intent on settling the boys and focused on this ultimate goal. But then, midway through the process, her attention seemed to dwindle. She would arrange to meet us and then cancel the appointment at the last minute. We no longer trusted that she was there for us. The meetings reverted to Spanish, and at times things moved quickly; but then at other times, nothing would happen for weeks or months.

One day, near the end of the process, Sara la Mala came to our house. (That was the day we started calling her that.)

'Hola. Are you well? How are the boys?' She had arrived late and was unpacking her bags as she walked towards our dining room table.

'We're good. The boys are at school. They are fine. They have learnt the alphabet now, but are having problems with learning words.'

'But Miguel? He is fine?'

'Yes, they both are.' I wondered why she kept asking, but we had a lot of work to get through before I had to pick up the boys from school.

Just before she left, Sara said a strange thing. 'When the process is finally over, I'll explain why I just asked about the boys.'

'What do you mean? Why can't you tell us now? Is something happening that we should know about?' I asked, feeling a flutter of nerves.

'No need for concern,' she said airily. 'There is nothing wrong. It is all going well.' But her eyes grew big as her mouth became tight.

'But, Sara, there must be something wrong. Otherwise, you wouldn't have brought it up. Please, this is so difficult for us. I'm sure you understand how we feel. Please tell us.'

For a moment, we tried to prevent her from leaving the house, but despite kidnapping being a regular occurrence in Mexico, it was not a good idea to take your own adoption lawyer hostage. Sara never divulged why she had highlighted that question. Not that day and not on any other day.

Finally, the day came when we were to sign the final documents. It had been eighteen months since the start of the adoption process. We had been dealing with the fallout of the premature closure of the orphanage and the traumatic homecoming for the boys. We'd been rejected and then reinstated as potential parents and we'd found a school, a therapist and some friends for the boys to play with. We'd been through eight weeks of labour in the form of court meetings, court hearings and court judgments. Adding our signatures to the final document was the last thread to be double-stitched before we could cut ties from the orphanage. Once this was done, we'd face the relatively simple hurdle of arranging our children's new birth certificates with our surnames on them.

We got dressed. We forced breakfast down our throats. Had a coffee and waited for Sara to arrive. We had some more coffee and carried on waiting. Sara la Mala was running late. She didn't call us. She just didn't turn up. Gradually, over the next two hours, I could feel the bile rise up into my throat. My heart was beating in my ears. It was getting more and more difficult to breathe. We tried to get hold of Sara but she was unavailable. Finally, after five hours of being kept in the dark, she called.

'It is already 2pm,' she told the Engineer. 'We'll sign the documents tomorrow.'

It was as if my waters had broken and my pregnant belly was desperate to push the babies out while the doctor was saying, 'I'm on the golf course, but it's okay. You can always push them out tomorrow.' I was listening to the one-sided conversation, butting in with urgent questions: 'What is she saying? Can we still go? Can we go without a lawyer? What is she saying?'

Suddenly the Engineer, who is usually calm and thoughtful, went white with rage. I hadn't seen that look too often and I took a step back.

There is an active volcano in Mexico called Popocatepetl which lies next to a mountain. The Aztec legend explains that Popocatepetl was a Náhuatl warrior who came home from war and found the love of his life dead. He sat down beside her and watched over her till the snow covered their bodies. Today, when the volcano sends fumes and ash into the air, the locals warn that Popo is angry.

That day, I could have sworn I saw smoke come out of Popo just before the Engineer had his last communication with Sara la Mala. I should have taken the phone from him when I saw him connect with this ancient anger. I heard the curse come forth with the quiet fury and vengeance of Popo behind him. The last thing he said to her was, 'Sara, I will pray for you. I will pray because I believe in the power of prayer and I believe that when someone prays with all their heart, things can come true. I will pray that one day, you understand the pain, suffering and anguish that you are putting us through. I will pray, and I will believe.'

Earlier in the year, I'd met someone in a Tai Chi class whose husband was an attorney. He accompanied us the next day to court. Someone we barely knew was prepared to drop everything so that we could end this eighteen-month-long pregnancy. It wasn't a problem that we didn't have Sara la Mala with us.

To Sara and the court, this was just another day at work. But to us, it marked the beginning of freedom.

CHAPTER 14

Music Tames the Beast

In the days preceding animal rights, a few smart people, led by Martin Seligman, decided to test a group of animals to see what would happen if they kept abusing them. The results became known as Learned Helplessness. The tests were done by electrical shocks being administered to dogs. Some got shocked and nothing hindered them, so they ran away. Some got shocked and could only run away if they pressed a lever. The last group was not given the opportunity to run away or stop the shocks. These dogs learnt that there was nothing they could do to help themselves, so they just sat down and whimpered. Later, even when they could have jumped over a small barrier to run away, they didn't. They could no longer trust the control handed to them. They had already given up.

Mexico is a country of treats and traumas. It is a country of hot Latin tempers and calm mystic mindfulness. In principle, Mexico loves its children so much that every year, at the end of April, a whole day is set aside for them.

The first time I experienced this homage was on our trip to Latin America. It was a Saturday and, while the Engineer was working, I went for a walk. A feeling of mass happiness permeated the streets. I was amid a fiesta in which policemen ran around with coloured confetti sticking to their uniforms after a playful attack of frivolity. Even I was accosted and eventually returned to our hotel with festive streaks of green and red in my hair.

When Miguel and Isaak joined the family, I wanted them to understand that fun could be part of life, but neither of the boys believed they were worthy of enjoyment. Amusements were stressful for them and positive reinforcement put them under pressure to perform. Even though the Engineer and I tried, we were not very successful with jovial family days because there was a cost to having serene merriment: it was usually followed by disheartening chaos. We had to measure out entertainment in small doses. Impromptu happiness was too dangerous for our family.

'Have you seen that when we play with Miguel, just as he starts to relax and have fun, once he notices that he's relaxing he gets angry?' the Engineer asked me.

'Yes, I have. He suddenly gets a scowl on his face and then soon after that, there is an argument or he does something he knows he shouldn't. The other day we were playing with the wooden blocks and he started leaning against me. Then when he realised that he'd relaxed into me, he just threw all the blocks up in the air and stormed off.'

I still had not been able to find anyone to help me understand what was going on, but I was sure that the happier Miguel became, the more difficult he made it for all of us.

Despite the harsh payback, the Engineer and I persisted. We managed bike rides to the park and ant-infested picnics. Outdoor soccer on thick-jacket cold days and indoor football on days when it was too hot to sit on plastic chairs. We even had rock-climbing days and adventurous early mornings when we drove to an airstrip and took lessons in glider planes. Movies and board games and a few quiet moments where we sat contentedly in a food coma, but we were constantly reminded that trust was not a natural state of being for our children.

'Isaak, ask her if we can play with the cars in the water again,' I heard Miguel whisper one day.

'Can we play with the water today?' Isaak asked me.

'Yes, of course you can,' I reassured him.

He needed further confirming. 'Can we put the cars in the water again?' he asked.

'Yes, the cars can go in the water,' I replied, wondering why Miguel didn't ask me himself.

I had come to realise that Isaak was often Miguel's speech vessel. I wondered if Miguel used this as a way of keeping me at bay or whether it was because he thought I'd respond more positively to Isaak.

Every kid deserves a try at a happy life, and every adult needs a break from stress, but our norm was a state of outburst. Remembering any moments of fun threatens to break me because they are fused with my failure to teach my children joy. But through the pain and struggles, there were a few times when we all had a good laugh.

When we first became a family, the boys were six-years-old. I would grasp small moments to try to make happy memories. Often, I'd lie down on the floor with my feet in the air and a boy's chest on my feet. 'Are you ready?' I would ask, and they always were ready. We'd play the helicopter game. I'd lift them into the air and swing them around and around. Bending my knees, with them hovering above me. Tipping and diving in those few moments of happiness, I didn't care that soon there would be a tantrum. In those moments, I was not making a mistake. I was not managing an unhappy or broken child. We were just one machine in a spare moment of bliss, flying around the room.

When I was young, my sisters and I would play records and dance around the room like maniacs. Some weekends my mother and father would join us, forgetting any hard times or that they may be angry with each other. We would all just move to the music. I loved watching my mother and father beep and bop to loud 70s and 80s pop music. Other times, wild African beats would get the family going. Sometimes I worried that the neighbours would send the cops to our door. I could imagine them complaining: 'Yes, officer, very inappropriate. And they dance to black-people music – they even get the little one doing it. Yes, officer, you must come as soon as possible.' Our shared enjoyment of the music would mould us into a family, a unit of one, and then once the music died down we would go back to being our separate selves.

Similarly, I tried to unite our little unit in Mexico with music. In our expat house surrounded by diplomats and dignitaries, I would play music loudly, and we would dance. I'd put Miguel or Isaak on my hip and I'd hold them close. We would dance and swing and jump around, toyi-toying to the music. Dipping them and twirling them fast as fast could dance. Johnny Clegg was often my go-to. He would tame the barbarian inside us. Those moments saved me. They saved us.

One day, driving with the boys, I found it hard to hold back the tears and, once again, I turned to Johnny Clegg. The music was too loud in the car, but it was either that or an emotional breakdown in the middle of the busy Mexican streets. Suddenly, from the back of the car, I heard two seven-year-olds singing at the top of their little Mexican lungs. In their never-before spoken English, they declared that they were 'scatterlings of Africa on a journey to the *staaarss*'.

This memory echoes in my mind. I hear their tiny voices belting out the words and my soul cries out for those small distraught humans. We were three specks on a planet hurtling along the busy Periférico ring road of chaos.

By the time the boys were seven, I had decided they should learn to ride a bike. My own failures in bike riding aside, I knew that I had to find an unconventional way to teach Miguel and Isaak. If they learnt too slowly, they would lose heart and think they weren't capable, but if I was not careful, they would resent me for helping them. The boys had been riding for quite some time using training wheels. In my dad's shop, we'd called them 'fairy wheels' and I realised that I could use this to bring some magic into the lessons.

One early pollution-free morning, we went to the park. It was quiet and our only company was a large dog who regarded us with droopy eyes. The sun shone through the trees, and we crunched leaves and twigs underfoot as we walked to the cracked and faded basketball court where kids rode their bikes. Spanner in hand, I shifted the fairy wheels slightly off the ground so that I could see which side each boy favoured. Then I sent the bikers out to ride. My tense muscles relaxed to the swooshing of the wheels on the ground while a bird or two tweeted around us. For a moment, my world was perfect and I wished time would stand still.

'Isaak, you are favouring the right fairy. I think she can come off now and fly free, don't you think?'

'Won't I fall?'

'No, she'll help you from the air if you need it. But you won't need it.' As I took the wheel off, I could see Isaak was sceptical, but soon he had automatically compensated his weight and was riding without using the remaining training wheel at all. The newest bike rider was born.

Miguel favoured his left wheel, but I was worried that if I took it off, he would feel out of control, so I tried something different.

'Miguel, your left fairy needs to work a bit harder. I'm going to take the right fairy away so that you can use the left one.'

'I don't need the fairy.'

'Okay, then in a few minutes I'll get rid of her too.'

With the bike leaning uncomfortably, Miguel naturally shifted his weight to the middle of the bike, and suddenly he was riding like a pro and puffed up with pride. The empowerment both boys received from learning to ride was amazing. Isaak was first to experience a big fall, and it was a doozey. He went flying over the handlebars and landed on all fours. I could see that he hadn't hurt himself too much so I clapped and shouted, 'Bravo, bravo!' My heart was in my throat though. I wanted to run up to him, cover him in protective kisses and never let a hard surface touch his skin again, but instead I jumped up and down as if he had won a medal in the Olympics.

'Well done. You had your first fall. It's the one we celebrate. Yay. Now you can have another trip around the court, and then we will go home. Yay.'

Miguel's turn came the following day. He came off in spectacular style, and I was there to clap and cheer him on even though I wanted to cover him with kisses too. This was one of the few times I could tell him he did a good job without him feeling burdened to maintain the performance. By not running along with them holding on to the bike, they had felt they had learnt on their own. The rub for me came when their friend asked them who showed them how to ride and the answer came: 'Just like you, my father taught me.'

That year's Mothers' Day, the Engineer made sure I got an extra-special gift from the boys. The complication of having to constrain my interest and care for my boys was always a challenge, but I learnt that childhood trauma affects more than just childhood.

In a way, I think learned helplessness was what happened to Isaak. He came to believe that there was nothing he could do to improve his life. He became so fixated on his pain as an infant that it became a part of him. He was no longer subject to abuse or neglect, and yet I still oversaw the day-to-day mechanics of his life. To this day he dreams of recouping his childhood or babyhood, but sadly, those days have passed and will not return.

I damn Mr Seligman because, while he was smart enough to discern the patterns of learned helplessness, he was not clever enough to 'cure' it once the damage had been done. I didn't need this experiment to understand that my sons fit the profile; I knew it before I read it. And there certainly was no victory when I could finally say, 'Ah, here it is. This is what happened.' I needed the broken glass *fixed*, but alas, there is no glue for this. Science had let me down. It let me down, and it let my sons down, leaving us on the floor snivelling and broken. All I had was knowledge. Broken, useless, unhelpful knowledge.

CHAPTER 15
The Sleeping Game

The Engineer and I had happily traded our gypsy lifestyle for school runs, homework, parent-teacher meetings, kid outings, kid movies, kid picnics, doctor appointments and, especially, late-night checks on the two people sleeping in the room next door to ours. I longed for either of my children to trust us enough to come out of their room and make an excuse to be with us. We would read a story and then cuddle up. Instead, when I lay down with one of my boys, it was like lying next to a rigid, frightened animal pretending to be asleep just to get rid of me.

The Engineer usually worked late into the night, but he has always been a good sleeper. I have never been. Sleep for me comes and goes at a whim. If I wake up in the middle of the night, no amount of counting sheep will get me back to the Land of Nod.

It was during those witching hours that I'd take advantage of the Engineer's calm nature. I'd wake him up with questions about multiplication sums, or I'd tell him, in an urgent whisper, 'Engineer, look at the moon.' Sometimes, illogically, I would wake him up because I couldn't see if he was breathing. He would take it all in his stride and sometimes even make me a cup of tea to keep me company and help me get back to sleep.

Isaak was a master of pretend sleep. He'd learnt in the toughest school around. I think he'd learnt how to 'sleep' even before he got to the orphanage where sometimes it was his best defence. In our house, he would be the first to fall asleep, his little chest rising and falling with slightly irregular breathing. Not too fast, not slow either. He took little breaks in the rhythm. Sometimes a bit deeper, sometimes a bit shallower. Face relaxed and body at ease. We would creep out of the room with the deep contentment of a job well done.

It was a good few months before I realised that Isaak was barely sleeping at all. It was the impromptu night experiments with the Engineer that helped me realise, for example, that when a person is asleep, they can feel a tickle. If a feather is used to gently tickle an ear, a sleeping person's hand will subconsciously push it away. I knew that Isaak was faking his sleep when I tickled his ear and he failed to respond. Even a kid who was a master at fake sleep didn't know all the tricks. It must have been hard for him to pretend that all was well and good when night-time brought monsters – and he had many monsters. Importantly, to him, all his monsters were human. In the torture house of my mind, I could only imagine that when he was an infant trying to survive, he'd had to teach himself to pass unnoticed.

Thriving infants, by contrast, are loved and learn that when they cry, someone comes to them. They learn that if they make a face while expelling wind, Mum will laugh: they control her heartstrings. From the earliest moments, babies learn the cause and effect of basic conversation. A cry, a hug. A cry, a hug. They should not be learning to pretend they are not there. They should not be learning that there is danger in a cry.

Isaak had clearly never experienced the give and take of baby conversations, of adult gurgles or smiles. Being ignored may have been a kinder outcome, but Isaak was not lucky enough to escape being ignored. The impact of this would manifest into his adult years in the name of reactive attachment disorder.

I often hear mothers complain that their kids will not stay in their bed at night. They emerge with a pretend tummy-ache, a need for water or simply want to sleep in Mum's bed. It's funny what we take for granted and what we get tired of.

The Engineer and I were never blessed with the pitter-patter of little feet coming into our bedroom; we never got angry because the kids would not stay in their room. I usually just smile when I hear parents complain. Sometimes I tell them they have no idea how I longed for my children to trust me enough to come to me in the middle of the night. Mostly, they think I don't understand their plight. I can't begin to tell them my story.

It was very difficult for Isaak not to unravel. He wasn't sleeping. He was pretending to be happy. He acted as though he was relaxed when nothing could have been further from the truth. This false persona was bound to crack; he could not maintain it indefinitely. Once he realised that he might be in a safe place, his little walls started to crumble, leaving him defenceless. We'd always been concerned that after all this time of his elaborate act, he would not know who he was. Slowly, we noticed that he simply did not have the strength to continue.

At first, I thought he was just tired. Then one day I came into the lounge to find him slowly sliding off the couch. He was staring blankly into vacant space. When I called his name, he blinked slowly and, equally slowly, pasted his fake smile on his face. Then he seemed to reanimate himself. His mask of happiness had been reinstated. From my limited medical knowledge at the time, I thought he was catatonic. It wasn't until much later that I could grasp that adoption isn't the fairy tale that I thought it was as a child. I think that day, as Isaak sat there looking into space, he was figuring it out too.

The sitting and staring grew into a habit. I spoke to the therapist about it, and we decided that he could be exhausted from the acts he'd been performing to make everyone happy. Now he'd reached a point of not knowing who he was, and not caring either. He just wanted to rest and think of nothing. There were days when he couldn't even pretend to listen.

'Isaak, sabes que? You know what? The sky is blue.'

'Yes.' His little voice sounded far away.

'Isaak, what colour did I say the sky was?'

'I don't know.'

I knew that he would not be able to tell me even if his life depended on it.

'I like your sweatshirt. Whose is it?' I asked.

'This sweatshirt belongs to Isaak,' he answered with no sense of self.

'I can see you are deep in thought now. What are you thinking of?'

'My brain is thinking of nothing.'

I tried everything I could think of to draw him out of this new shell.

When adopting older kids, there is a risk that the child will attach to a therapist rather than the parent. For this reason, our family therapist saw the boys only occasionally. Instead, the Engineer and I took the bulk of the sessions. She taught us how to be the therapist for our children. Our therapist told us to trust our instinct. She told us that Isaak was not in any danger and there was no right or wrong way to deal with this new problem. He just needed time.

I got more and more worried. Trust my instinct? Well, my instinct was that this child needed an emotional outlet and if he didn't get one, he would never heal. I tried every soft way to show him he was in a safe place and that he would be okay, but nothing worked. He simply had a deficit of trust.

Then one day, without much thought, I put him on my lap and softly said to him in Spanish, 'You are okay, and you need to speak to me.' When he did not respond, I asked him again, and again. Finally, frustrated and scared shitless for him, I just yelled, 'SPEAK TO ME.' The long slow wail that came out of this tiny mouth was heart wrenching. For the first time, he started to cry, and he cried, and cried. The dam wall had burst. We sat on the floor, both of us crying, while I cradled him in my arms.

Whenever I relay this story to others I'm asked how I could've been so heartless. I am told that I was cruel. All I can say is, 'I wear size eight-and-a-half shoes. When you want to walk in them, let me know and I'll lend them to you.'

I did it because I believed my son's life depended on it. I continued to shout at him until he cried because that was the only language he understood, and even if it broke my heart, I knew that he needed to get the emotion out. And out it came. I did it until one day he came and asked me to please make him cry. At that point, I told him with all the love in my mother-heart, 'Of course, I'll make you cry, sweetie, but this is the last time. From now on we need to find a better way for you to get rid of your sad emotions.' And then I proceeded to make him cry one last time. By this time he only needed a half-hearted, 'Do you want to cry? Why do you want to cry? Speak to me.' After that, he would find other ways to deal with a build-up of emotion.

Throughout his life, Isaak would continue not to trust the Sandman, and to this day sleep doesn't come easily to him. The impact of this on his psyche is profound, and partly responsible for his ongoing processing disorder.

New mothers and fathers caring for their children around the clock don't need books or research to be aware of the powerful effects of sleep deprivation. How much more so for Isaak's young developing mind?

He had been abandoned, abused, traumatised. He had attachment disorder, developmental delays, abandonment issues, PTSD and for all we knew, Foetal Alcohol Syndrome. He could not internalise that he was a person worthy of the opportunities he was receiving. At times, he didn't even know that he *was* a person. Where Miguel had impulse-control issues and rage, Isaak lacked motivation to do anything and had no energy to recognise an emotion.

When you are dealing with kids who have endured an unimaginable beginning in life, you desperately want love to conquer all. After all, it's the myth we are constantly fed: *Love will conquer all. Love saves. And they all lived happily ever after.* Except it doesn't really, does it? Disney and all the others are wrong. Sometimes love is not enough; sometimes all the love in the universe is not enough to put Humpty Dumpty and his adoptive brother back together again.

But we were determined to try.

CHAPTER 16
Swim, Said the Mama Fishie

Meeting our children at the age of six meant that, unlike most parents, we still had to get to know them. Soon after our children moved in with us, the Engineer was standing waist-deep in our friends' swimming pool while I sat on the edge, dipping my feet into the cool water.

'I learnt to swim at the same time as the older kids at the home,' Isaak said, only half convincingly. 'I'm very good. I don't need help.' He was calmly sitting in an inflatable boat with a big smile on his face. The Engineer was at the ready in case he needed to catch a drowning child.

Just then, the boat slowly flipped over and Isaak started to sink towards the bottom of the pool. The Engineer pulled him up like a dead rat.

'Oops, I guess you can't swim after all,' he said.

'No, but I have had a lesson,' Isaak said, trying to maintain his fake smile while figuring out why he had suddenly gone *glug-glug-glug* towards the bottom of the pool.

The following weekend we went to a resort with a swimming pool so that we could teach the boys how to swim. As soon as we arrived, the

Engineer and the boys jumped into the pool. For the rest of the morning he tried to teach them how to put their heads under water. This is never an easy task, and much harder when there is limited trust.

In my case, the adage '*Those who can, do; those who can't, teach*' is true. As a three-year-old, I knew how to swim; but when we moved to a house without a pool, I quickly forgot. At the age of six, I once refused to jump into the pool at school. My teacher picked me up and threw me in. I went into a tailspin, making the situation much worse. It wasn't that I didn't want to swim; it was that I no longer knew how. It was at that point we all realised that sometimes a child's fear overrides what an adult thinks they know (a lesson I would have done well to remember as a mother). I never quite got over my fear of water, no matter how many lessons I had. The experience gave me an interesting perspective on learning to swim.

'Okay, I'm tired of listening to this,' I said that day at the resort. 'Everyone get out the pool right now. I'm going to teach you how to swim.'

The three of them gave me weird looks. The Engineer shook his head, shrugged his shoulders, and with no small measure of relief, went in search of a cold fruit juice. The boys lay on the warm tiles at the edge of the pool.

'Okay, so listen. I don't mind if you breathe out through your nose or your mouth. For now, you choose. It is important to learn how to put your face under water without drowning.' Two pairs of brown eyes looked up at me. 'So here is a trick. Things are always easier if you know how to keep your eyes open. You are safe here outside of the pool. Take a deep breath and pop your head under. Slowly let your breath out, and as you let the air out of your nose or your mouth, look at my fingers. When you have no more air to let out, lift your head out the water and tell me how many of my fingers you saw. Make sure you don't breathe in when your nose and mouth are under water. Ready?'

'But I thought you said you'd show us how to swim?' Miguel said accusingly.

'I will. But I think the problem is that you don't trust that you won't drown. Lying here on the warm tiles, you are safe and you don't need to worry about all that. If you get scared, you pop your head out. Okay, got it? Those are the rules.'

When they were ready, they carefully put their heads in the water.

'Three fingers!' Isaak shouted as bubbles popped where his head had been.

'No, silly, don't guess. Just open your eyes and tell me what you see.'

'Five. I see five fingers.'

Pretty soon, they felt comfortable breathing out under water with their eyes open.

'Okay, guys, the rest is just learning to flap your arms and kick your legs correctly. Let's get in and try some kicks. When we get back to Mexico City, I'll find a swimming teacher,' I said as I wandered off to find a suitable celebratory cocktail for myself.

It was another reminder that I would constantly have to find innovative ways to teach my children. I only hoped I was up to the task.

CHAPTER 17

Chocolates: A Weapon of Choice

Once I'd made the transition from kindergarten to the long-awaited 'big' school, I thought I was set for life. In fact, it was the first of many lessons about chasing an end goal. I soon realised that big school was just another beginning.

On my first day, a reporter from the local newspaper came and took pictures of us. Ours was the first Grade One class in what was previously a high school. We were the experiment that no one was ready for. After the reporter had made notes, the photographers had taken pictures and the speeches ended, the high school students went back to their classrooms. Ten little boys and four little girls dressed in handmade uniforms sat under a tree for our first lesson à la *Little House on the Prairie*. I always look back on those early school days with fondness and a bit of pioneering pride. We were the first, and would continue to be the first, until we reached high school.

Finding the right school for my own children turned out to be an experiment too. The Engineer and I had chosen a Montessori school close to his office because we were drawn to the philosophy of pressure-free learning; it seemed to fit with what we thought we knew about our sons. Our two little people had been through a lifetime of pressure and they were only six years old. We didn't want to add further challenges to their learning experience.

The problem came when the teachers noticed that once the boys had learnt something new, they regressed. Our streetwise kids had worked out quickly that learning didn't stop after mastering the first task. They promptly rejected the whole education idea. Rather, they held firm to the belief that once you learnt the alphabet, you shouldn't have to learn words as well. It was no fault of the teachers. It was no fault of the system. It was their determined view that ignorance is bliss. The boys were already behind in their education and we were aware that time was running out. So with sadness, we went in search of a mainstream school. And that was how I came to give a school psychologist a vengeful gift of … chocolates.

We visited a few schools and found the one we liked most. We watched the mail and listened for the phone until one day news arrived. The boys had been approved. Elated, the Engineer and I stopped what we were doing and attended the placement interview, chequebook in hand. A few more interviews and a substantial drop in our bank balance later, we found ourselves sitting in front of a heavyset school psychologist who had slightly overdone the perfume and the jewellery that morning.

It soon became evident that Señora SchoolPsycho seemed determined to demonstrate her judgemental, racist and elitist side. With her bright-red lipstick and nails, she showed no empathy towards our boys who, in these surroundings, were outliers. She was about to wield her power over my brown little boys, and it was quite clear that she saw them as inferior. Smugly, she asked all kinds of questions that did not relate to the boys or the school, but I put up with her interrogation for the sake of my boys.

'Where did you grab these boys from?' Her tone made me feel as if they were dirty bags in the street.

'We met in an orphanage where I was volunteering.'

'Did you try many times to fall pregnant? Wouldn't you have preferred to have your own?'

'These are my children and they are waiting to get into this school.' She was awakening the lioness in me, but it was not until her final question that I lost my patience.

'Why did you decide to adopt these boys?'

My control had worn a little too thin. I had been through all the questions relating to the adoption with lawyers, psychologists and social workers, judges and clerks, home visits and house invasions. Now I refused to face a similar interrogation from a closed-minded school psychologist.

'Why do you need to know the reasons for adopting our children?' I asked quietly, trying to prevent my fingers from clenching into a fist.

'It will help me understand the boys and which class we put them into,' she said.

'I don't understand. I think the music we play in our house has more of an effect on their behaviour than our *reason* for adopting them. Our reasons have no bearing on which class they should go into and has nothing to do with the school.'

'But we simply need to know. Don't take offence.'

'Their needs and personality might be influenced by the *fact* that they are adopted, but not the reason they joined our family.' By now, I'd lost my grasp on calmness. I can't remember if I threw in an F-bomb but I do remember the horrified look on the receptionist's face as I stormed out of the office, leaving the Engineer to sort things out.

To this day, I do not think it was an appropriate question, but I realised that I'd need to suck it up for the sake of my boys and that I'd have to apologise. And apologise I did. I suppose I could have written a heartfelt note, except I really wouldn't have been able to pull off the heartfelt part. I could have given her flowers, but flowers were too pretty and I wasn't really sorry. I sat at home, boiling over with rage, when I remembered overhearing her say to the receptionist that she had just started a diet.

It was the last box of chocolates I ever gifted to anyone. After that, I couldn't, in good faith, bring a box of extra hip and thigh to my friends. Chocolates as gifts would be tainted forever.

Not being a confident Spanish reader, I bought some beautifully illustrated children's books that came with audio discs. The stories were narrated to background classical music: stories of Bach, Beethoven and Mozart. Whenever the Engineer wasn't home in time to read to the boys they would take turns to choose an audiobook.

I had been hoping that by the time I went to Australia for a family function, the adoption process would be over, and they could join me. Unfortunately, I had to explain to Miguel and Isaak that they would be staying in Mexico with the Engineer while I visited family overseas. The boys took it in their stride, so I was surprised when I got a call from Señora SchoolPsycho who summoned me for a meeting.

'I have to tell you that both your boys are obsessed with death. Obsessed.' Today her lipstick was bright pink, perfectly matching the bird pattern on her blouse.

'Death? That hasn't come up with us. How did you find this out?' I asked, a little bewildered.

'They have been drawing pictures of winged people flying in a big city. When I asked what they drew, they told me it was a city full of angels.'

'Oh, I've been telling them that I will fly through the city of Los Angeles to visit my sister in Australia. It didn't occur to me that in Spanish, Los Angeles means "the angels".'

'I don't think it's that at all,' she replied haughtily. 'When I asked your sons if they knew anyone who had died, the boys told me that they knew

Bach, Beethoven and Mozart were dead. See, they are only interested in the dead.' As she leaned back into her leather chair, her eyes closed for a long second. She seemed to be relishing this.

'I understand the problem,' I said. 'My Spanish reading isn't good, so I bought audiobooks about Bach, Beethoven and Mozart. I think there is a misunderstanding because of the way I said "city of the angels" – you know, Los Angeles. I must have said it wrong. They are just drawing what I said.'

'I am sitting here and telling you that your children are obsessed with death. They need therapy.'

I was coming very close to having to gift her another box of chocolates but I managed to control myself. Señora SchoolPsycho never fully relinquished that one, and it haunted us a few more times. But I was willing to bet that for all the issues my children had, death was not one of them.

CHAPTER 18
African Game

'I'm following the ambulance to the hospital.' I was trying to focus on the distant voice on the other end of the phone. 'When we went to visit your dad this morning, he couldn't breathe. I think he'll be okay once we get him settled. I'm sorry to give you this difficult news.'

I was already packing as I put the phone down. I started delegating my fingers as one hand dialled my sister's number and the other paged through my directory looking for the travel agent's details. I had just been woken up by the ringing phone and it was going to be a long day.

My father's emphysema wasn't the problem. It was the discovery of cancer we were concerned about. My father had known doctors from the early age of thirteen when his own father went into the hospital for a stomach complaint and never came out.

To a child, it may have seemed unfair; and at some point while he was figuring out how to be the man of the house, he began to believe that doctors don't always get it right. As sometimes happens in life, this turned out to be a prophecy for my father himself.

'Don't come yet. The chemo will be fine,' he had said. 'Better to stay away until I need you.'

This had made sense, so I'd stayed away until that early morning phone call.

He'd told me that the doctor had given him about an eighty per cent chance of recovery before the chemo. I had been concerned but not worried. I stayed in Mexico. A few days before he went in for chemo, he caught a cold. The doctor told him this wouldn't be a problem so he went in for his first round. It turned out to be his last.

I flew the long journey from Mexico to Brazil to South Africa, all the while hoping and praying to a god I no longer believed in that I would make it home in time to see my dad. Death was kind to me and waited. He waited until my sisters and I all arrived and then, once He knew that we were not waiting for anyone else, He took my father by the hand and led him to the big bowling green in the sky.

Soon after the funeral, the Engineer and the boys joined me in South Africa. The Engineer helped me pack up my dad's house and the month we spent there was bittersweet. It was the first time my extended family were getting to meet my sons. We had only recently officially become a family even though we had been living together for about a year and a half. There was joy and sadness mixed in with all the emotions that accompany the passing of a father. I didn't want my children to associate South Africa with death, sadness and packing up so we arranged a trip to a game park for the boys to see wild animals.

It wasn't until we arrived at the Kruger National Park that we realised we had led the boys to expect a completely different type of getaway. We were looking out for animals, whereas the boys were looking out for slides, swings, climbing castles, labyrinths and board games or dress ups. Having grown up in South Africa, we never went on 'safari'. That word called to mind travelling caravans of pompous Englishmen in pith helmets and slaves setting up high tea in white china cups, vast expanses of landscapes and delicate women taking ill along the African trade routes from Cape to Cairo. Our colloquial use of the term 'game park' led Miguel and Isaak to think we'd played a trick on them. Thankfully, they got over their disappointment quickly and soon we were driving along, looking for the next animal sighting.

It was on the second day that Miguel shouted from the back of the car, 'Look! An idiot!' He was excitedly pointing at a tourist who had thoughtlessly put his life in danger by posing for a photograph next to a group of monkeys. Growing up, the Engineer and I had often heard stories of foreigners being eaten by lions as they posed for the camera or being attacked by baboons. It was a small surprise to me that Miguel had been listening when I told him not to roll down the windows.

Driving through the game reserve was a healing time for me. For the boys, it was an amazing experience to see raw nature. Ferocious and gentle, merciless and sympathetic all at once.

When an eight-year-old sits in a car for hours on end, they usually get bored. When there are two of them, the back seat of the car can get interestingly loud, to say the least, but we found Miguel and Isaak surprisingly patient and at ease as we drove along looking out for animals. We had spot-the-hippo games, and now and then tried to trick each other into looking for animals that just don't exist in Africa. It remains one of the rare times in our lives together that we had very few disagreements for more than a couple of hours at a time.

Although we had a couple of spats, we avoided family wars. The boys had come, so it seemed, to some unannounced truce with the Engineer and me.

Naturally, we thought we were making progress, but it turned out that they were saving their familiar meltdowns for our return to Mexico.

Once back home I found that in an odd way, they had a new reason for their deep-down resentment of me. They blamed me for not letting them meet the only living person they would have been able to call abuelo, grandfather.

CHAPTER 19

The Silence

Silence is golden, they say, and Isaak liked silence. Wherever we go in the world, people comment on my golden boy who is so quiet. But Isaak used silence as a weapon, so for me, silence became plutonium. It tarnished quickly and accumulated in the bones.

At first, I thought he was just a quiet child, but then I realised that he created the silence especially for me. He knew how to wield it, brandishing it to keep me at a distance and to contain me behind a wall where he had decided I belonged. I worried that one day he might explode, and if that detonation ever came, I feared it would destroy him.

When I was still quite young, my eldest sister's boyfriend would visit our house on the weekend. We would all go into the 'big' lounge and wait with him while she got ready for their date. Sometimes the conversation would fall away, and we'd sit in silence. Being the youngest in the house meant that my typical day was very different from the rest of the family. I was used to a lot of quiet time, and found silence was a solitary beauty. I was comfortable with it when I was alone, but sitting in the quiet lounge with others was disconcerting. I felt there had to be sound. I would laugh my mad little head off at the stillness blanketing us together. The quieter and more uncomfortable everyone else became, the funnier I would find it. My middle sister would scowl at me and the more she did that, the more I would laugh.

So you see, Isaak and I instinctively came from different sides of silence. He loved silence when he was with other people, but I didn't.

I confessed my misgivings about Isaak to our family therapist.

'Oh, are you sure you aren't being a bit sensitive?' she asked me in her motherly way. Her office was homely and fitted well with adults and children alike.

'Is there a way to check? You know, sniff it out for a trace of plutonium? Chat with him and see his reaction?'

She smiled at my joke. 'I'll see what's there,' she said, putting down her notebook to indicate our meeting was over.

Two weeks later she reported back to me. She'd risen to the challenge and tackled the question between bouts of drawings. She asked Isaak if he ever ignored me on purpose.

'Yes,' he said. 'All the time.'

'Aren't you scared that one day she will ignore you too?'

'No,' he replied. 'I have tried it often. When I want to ignore her, I ignore her and when I want something and I talk to her, she always answers. It works well for me.' His methods were that of a ninja specialised in unorthodox arts of war, not letting ethics or honour stand in his way of combat.

Isaak was a quiet fighter. He was a gentle and careful warrior with a secret and mindful power. It wasn't only the silence. It was his determination too – which became evident during his karate tournaments. He hated the katas and I can honestly say he didn't enjoy the fights either; but there was something very natural about his performance in the tournaments.

When I took him for his first lesson in the dojo, he feared the shouting from the students as they punched the air. He did not like noise and he was not a violent child, but we sensed karate might help him release some of his fear-filled emotions so we gave it a try. Soon he was loving the classes, and when his first tournament came around and he smashed it, we realised that he was hooked.

In Mexico, they practise contact karate. None of the 'stop the punch before you get to the skin' type of martial art that we're accustomed to in our soft English-speaking countries. No. There they teach you to punch like you mean it and then maintain the momentum. Move your fist into the middle of your target. Punch like you are in trouble and punch as if your life depends on it because one day, in the middle of Mexico City, your life may depend on it. Although the students do wear some awesome-looking protection, there are a lot of open body spaces to hit.

The Engineer and I would attend these tournaments, ulcers forming in our stomachs and hearts beating jungle songs in our throats. One match stood out. I knew we were in for a different experience when we arrived to find Goliath's son standing in the Under 9 age group. He was a vindictive fighter and I watched him annihilate every one of his opponents. Isaak was short and stocky, and Goliath's son wore a smirk on his heavyset face that scared me – and I was not even on the mat. When I heard his trainer say, 'Okay, let's finish this one quickly.' I almost stopped the match before it started.

As the bell rang out and I was still inhaling deeply, Son of Goliath rushed in and did a high kick. The tournament had rules to protect the kids, and kicks to the head were firmly disallowed. Isaak moved out of the way and won two points. Son of Goliath was not happy and neither was his coach. The giant was seeing red and his coach instructed him to 'aim well'. From then on things moved very quickly. The coach's face broke into a tyrannical smile and then, in slow motion, my boy hit the mat with a huge thump, where he lay, struggling to breathe. The entire room came to a standstill. People who hadn't even been paying attention stopped to see what would happen next.

Isaak got up, still breathing hard and with tears in his eyes. I ran towards him, shouting at him to stop the fight. It was not worth it. The judge got out of his seat and went down to Isaak. Face to face, he spoke very clearly and very softly, telling him there was no shame in stepping away. The judge, however, did not know that Isaak had been in worse situations. Hell, not even *I* knew at that stage.

Slowly, really slowly, Isaak dabbed tears from his eyes, took a deep breath and wiped his snot on his sleeve. 'I am ready,' he said carefully, with me still shouting in the background.

I saw Son of Goliath's coach nod. He looked excited. His boy was going to win this one. He winked at his protégé and said, as if to a bullfighter, 'Matalo.' (Kill him.)

As Isaak stepped back onto the mat, his classmates from the dojo began a low chant: 'I-saak. I-saak. I-saak. I-saak.' I stopped and looked around at the Engineer. It felt like I was in a movie. Wax on, wax off. This was the real thing. 'I-saak. I-saak. I-saak.' The chant was taken up by the whole dojo group. 'I-saak. I-saak. I-saak.' Then parents joined in. 'I-saak. I-saak. I-saak.' Now everyone, except the kids in Goliath's class, was shouting. A few mothers wiped tears from their eyes. Isaak stepped onto the mat and suddenly it was as if a light went on. This was the flight or fight kind of moment he was made for.

The fight was over and Isaak's classmates were carrying *my* child on their shoulders, big smile on his sad little eight-year-old face, trophy in hand. I was still stunned by what had happened.

Goliath said nothing, disappointed in his son's performance. Goliath's son slunk away in defeat. As for his coach, he came up to Isaak and shook his hand.

CHAPTER 20
Big in Japan

When the Engineer had to go to Japan on business for eight weeks, the school agreed that it would be a great education for two nine-year-old boys to see the world. With some pre-arranged schoolwork packed so the boys wouldn't fall behind, we joined the Engineer in Tokyo for the last two weeks of his trip.

Each day after midday we had fun, but before then it was a battle to get Miguel to do his schoolwork for the day. Originally, we planned to do half an hour in the morning and half an hour in the evening, but I soon learnt that it was better to endure one fight a day than two. Miguel's screaming and banging was so intense I feared someone would knock on the door suspecting to find a murder scene. The afternoons, however, were extraordinary.

While the Engineer was at work, we travelled around Tokyo and the surrounding areas, discovering new ideas and a completely different culture. The people we met were kind and generous; wherever we went, the boys received gifts. Teenage girls would request photographs with them as though they were celebrities. They were treated like little princes.

One day, on a train packed full of people with only two seats remaining, I stood while the boys sat. When an elderly lady got on the train, I asked the boys to share a seat. But the lady refused to sit. She shook her head vigorously and pointed to their feet, gesturing the universal sign for 'small'. Then she pointed to her own feet and showed me that they were big. She picked up my child, who was now squashing his brother, and plopped him back on his seat. She taught me that respect is important, but the simple truth is that small kids have small feet and can't stand comfortably for a long time.

The boys and I filled our days with temples, tempura and train rides. At each temple or shrine, Miguel eagerly followed the custom at the gate. He performed a little bow, scooped the flowing water with the bamboo ladle and poured it over his left hand, then his right. He'd wipe his little mouth with his wet hands and tip the remaining water out the ladle. Once he'd 'cleansed' himself, he would pass the ladle to Isaak, who copied him, and then it was my turn. I began to wonder if my little boy was a Shinto or Buddhist monk at heart.

One weekend, the Engineer and I took the boys to a toyshop that spanned five floors. Mechanical toys, computer toys, simple toys. If it was a game or had a button or made a strange sound, it was there.

'Boys, grab a basket and fill it with toys. Anything on this floor is an option,' the Engineer said, getting caught up in the excitement of the store and its prices. As the boys ran off to get their baskets, faces lit up with exhilaration, I started to question the wisdom of this generous offer. I was worried that we wouldn't be able to afford two baskets full of toys, not to mention the extra luggage charge we would incur at the airport.

As it turned out, my fears were unfounded. In fact, I was a little heartsore when the boys came back having selected the smallest and cheapest thing they could find. Evidently, we would have to teach them 'to be dirty' all over again. Unlike many other kids who demand everything in sight, our boys had learnt to manage their expectations in order to avoid disappointment. Schooled in deprivation, they could not easily grasp that you can never have too many toys.

I decided they needed a lesson in retail therapy so together we walked around the store, choosing whatever grabbed our attention. I knew my boys still feared kindness and, from previous experience, I was sure there would be a backlash to all the giving. Another illogical tantrum. But for that morning, we were just an ordinary family sharing some laughs in a toyshop.

Our Japanese trip was wonderful and crushing in equal measure. The harrowing mornings followed by spectacular afternoons wore me down. I was starting to accept that there might never be a simple path for my post-institutionalised children, but I did glimpse some hope of happiness for us all. By the end of the trip, I knew that while I might not have managed to give my children comfort at night or care in the day, I had been able to give them a learning experience that most kids dream of. As for the rest – I would keep trying to get it right.

CHAPTER 21

Without Brakes

For their first six years of life, our children had used adrenalin to survive. We realised that we needed to give them quick adrenalin-release opportunities which would help them express a build-up of frustration and anger. So I hung a punching bag in the entrance of our home. Anyone could put on gloves and punch or kick the hell out of it. Simply knowing that there was something to hit somehow allowed the stress to dissipate. Activities that allowed a flight-or-fight response seemed to be healing.

The Engineer often went rock climbing with a Brazilian friend named Wes. It didn't take long before the boys joined them. Wes explained what to do, and with a couple of demonstrations, Isaak started climbing like a hybrid monkey-goat-boy. He went up thirty metres before the rope ran out. Every move he made, every decision he took was like a pro. He was totally in the moment. He had finally found a use for the adrenalin he kept at the ready for potentially dangerous moments. Miguel was also impressive. He went up three metres and then found his comfort level.

Soon enough, the boys started nagging us to go rock climbing every weekend. We bought them their own harness and Wes gave them a chalk bag. I also found release on those days. Once the boys had left – rope, helmet and chalk bag in hand – I would head to the couch and grab my chance to stare at nothing.

By now, our boys had travelled to Africa and Japan. They had seen the wonders of lions and elephants in the wild, visited famous temples and giant shopping centres. But most of their classmates had been to the beach resort of Puerto Vallarta and they hadn't. Even if a person has eaten caviar, they sometimes still crave the taste of a simple burger. Soon, with all the talk about that area, even the Engineer and I wanted to go, and so we booked a holiday at the popular haven. We chose a resort with a beach, a pool and a kids' club but there were so many exciting activities in the area that we were hardly at the hotel. In fact, we barely saw the pool and the boys didn't even make it to the kids' club. We were up for every experience we could pack into a day: zip-lining across treetops, swimming with dolphins. We knew that the more fun we had on holiday, the greater the risk of tantrums and resistance upon our return, but for one week we basked in a halcyon-type calmness.

In true life-lesson manner, the highlight of our trip also underscored our predicament as adoptive parents. It happened the day we went dune-buggy driving. The buggy was a tiny two-seat go-cart with no floor. It had a VW engine, and red and blue metal tubes instead of a roof. In Mexico, safety regulations were often just a guideline and protection was optional.

'Here are the keys and maybe you can find a helmet on the wall if one fits you. Don't take your feet off the metal bars, amigos. Now all you need to do is follow Ricardo. He's the leader.'

Ricardo turned out to be a maniac with no fear. A true Aztec. We followed him onto the highway, where people were driving their cars and trucks at over 120 km/h. The road hurtled under our bums as we saw and felt each pebble we drove over. Finally, we arrived at a farm where we were given a few minutes to enjoy the surroundings and a moment to gather ourselves.

'Pull your nerves and your stomach back to where they should be, cabrón – and don't worry if you shat yourself, güey. Soon nobody will notice because next, we drive through rivers and cow paddocks. You'll all be covered in shit anyway, amigos.' Ricardo laughed at his own joke and slammed his foot on the accelerator.

The Engineer and I followed with a kid in each buggy, doing our best to keep up with the rest of the group. Suddenly I realised things were about to get very interesting. My buggy started to go faster and faster down the sloping sand ravine. My brakes were on a break. The Engineer was in front of me and I needed space to overtake him. But there was no space. I had no hooter either. My brain froze; we were going to crash and Miguel was sitting next to me.

I did the only thing I could. I let out a high-pitched scream and threw a protective arm across Miguel. I don't know what the Engineer thought when he heard my vocal hooter, but he swerved out of my way and stopped as I overtook him at a stupidly fast speed and drove to the top of the ravine where my buggy finally lost momentum and came to a stop in a bush. The other drivers were still following the leader, so far ahead that they had no idea of our predicament.

Miguel looked at me with excitement in his eyes. 'That was fun! Why did you scream and put your arm out in front of me?'

'Oh, because I wanted to get the Engineer out the way and I didn't have a hooter.'

Fun was imitating life: just as our car had no brakes, neither did our lives. We were hurtling along a cow paddock, getting the shit kicked up in our faces, doing our best to enjoy the ride and holding on for all we were worth.

If we could have installed a permanent side order of danger and adrenalin for our children in their everyday lives, they might have had a better chance of enjoying the calmer times. Instead, it seemed we were always in search of failed dune buggies and monoliths to climb.

CHAPTER 22

Not My Mexico

I've always felt that we should never judge anyone based on only one of their stories. Looking back on the chaotic day when we were almost arrested, I was reminded of this. No matter who we are, we are all complex beings. Each of our experiences reveals a different facet of who we are in any given moment. In my father's shop, I was the seller of paint, the taker of money and the giver of change. I was a semi-bilingual speaker and a DIY pro. In school, I was a target. A shy, nondescript hanger-on. A slow learner and a watcher, not a doer. Victim in one place, berserker in another.

By the time of our detainment, Mexico had utterly enchanted me. Both the good and the bad would make me smile, no matter where I was. I loved the people, the colours, sights, sounds, smells. I even loved the wild and unpredictable traffic.

But the day at the police station changed my narrative: Mexico was no longer *my* Mexico anymore. From that day on I started looking over my shoulder all the time. The Engineer and I became aware of how much our family stood out and the danger those differences posed for our boys.

'Do you know these people? Why are you with them?'

'These are my parents.'

That scene played itself out for me on a repetitive loop.

One thing I have always known about my boys is that they are tough, and due to their early-life experiences, their decision-making abilities are very distinctive. The detainment episode showed me a different story when it came to Isaak. We had seen how he'd dealt with adversity in a karate tournament, but this was the first time we'd witnessed him come alive in the face of a life-changing menace. He switched from victim to survivor in an instant. His challenging start in life had trained him well for this moment. It marked the opening of the puzzle that was Isaak. It answered the question: what happened before we knew what happened? It indicated, in the most blatant way, that this little boy had been endangered very early on. Danger was his reset button. His path to peak performance.

'Do you know these people? Why are you with them?'

'These are my parents.'

That fateful day when our interrogators escorted us to the police station, our request for a Human Rights representative calmed the situation down. We were no longer dealing with Oblong-glasses. Instead, we were dealing with a new guy, a skinny man with shifty eyes and a white spot on his mouth.

'I will help sort this out for you. I have called the Human Rights department.'

I didn't believe him.

Isaak sat on the back seat of the car, comfortably strong. The Engineer collected himself. Miguel, however, sat staring into the void. His story had changed too. Most of the time Miguel was like a Comanche fighter, a warrior believing his life depended on each fight. But today, for the first time, he was quiet, trying to be smaller than he was. His lessons in abuse taught him that in times of danger it is best to either be aggressive or hide. Sitting in the back of the car on that day, Miguel knew that aggression was not his best choice so the impulse to hide took over. He became the victim. In the midst of this bedlam, he simply shut down.

He didn't know how to react and so he didn't.

'Do you know these people? Why are you with them?'

'These are my parents.'

When the Hugh Jackman-esque motorcyclist arrived sporting his Dogs and Cats black T-shirt and wearing no helmet, it didn't take us long to comprehend that he was not from the Human Rights department at all. WhiteSpot had called in a colleague. A new game had begun and we had no choice but to play it through.

After a few questions, some notes and a short word with the kids, DogandCat astutely assessed the situation. He said he had called the office and verified our story about adopting the kids. He'd managed the impossible feat of confirming our story in ten minutes. On a Sunday morning. From a street in Mexico City. All this from a disorganised, computerless office that was, most importantly, closed on the weekend. Once again, we were reminded of how the officials were often a law unto themselves, but we were not going to argue with his facts now that we were free to go. The drama had played out and ended.

Some might say it was an anticlimax. Others might say we were lucky. For us, it was just another unexpected thing that came our way. Our children had survived unthinkable experiences. We had been through so many obstacles, fought so many fights and had so much stress thrust upon us, that by the time we were entrapped and released, it was just another interesting morning.

'Do you know these people? Why are you with them?'

'These are my parents.'

Mostly, I was the one who was always confronted about our children. People stopped me in the shopping centre to ask me when I would be taking the boys back to their parents, or they asked the kids who I was or even where their mother was while I was standing right next to them. The Engineer's story changed on that day too. For the first time, he could also see how we stood out.

That day our tale changed. We'd gone out looking for a pair of sneakers, and the fallout for the day was that it would be another twelve years before our sons would be comfortable putting Converse on their feet again.

A month after our attempted arrest, two other people's story also changed. The people in question were narcotics policemen in plainclothes taking pictures of a drug deal outside a Mexican school. Some parents perceived a different scenario. They saw two guys planning a kidnapping. Soon the narcotics police were surrounded by angry parents and what followed was nothing less than slaughter. The policemen were literally pulled apart limb from limb. By the time their backup arrived, their burnt bodies lay in the sand. Their story highlighted how well ours had ended. Perhaps next time it wouldn't. If I was sure of anything, it was that there would be a next time for us.

I had learnt all types of survival skills. I had grown accustomed to taking different routes in and out of our suburb. I knew not to get into my car if a van was parked too close to the driver's side. I had learnt that if ever I was in danger, to kick the knees, poke the eyes and use my elbows. The average mother shouldn't need to know these things.

Each day came with a new story of violence, corruption or kidnapping. News articles began appearing about policemen from the department that investigated kidnappings who were also running one of the biggest kidnapping organisations in Mexico at the time. A little boy in our street had been kidnapped getting onto the school bus with his minder. He was held for a few days until his parents could collect enough money to pay the ransom. A little girl was taken and held for months. Her parents knew if they paid for her too quickly, it could happen again. The child of a janitor who worked for an international company was stolen. He had no money, but the company helped him pay, as the kidnappers knew they would. Everywhere we looked, children were in danger.

I was acutely aware of the spotlight on us: we were gringos, the Engineer worked for an international company, we lived in a good neighbourhood, our children were not the same colour as us. And we had almost been arrested for kidnapping. We stood out. We drew unwanted attention constantly. I felt like we were a target on both sides of the wall. I loved my Mexico, but the signs were no longer whispers in the dark. We needed to make a change.

'Do you know these people? Why are you with them?'

'These are my parents.'

On that Sunday the story changed, and in the process, it changed us.

A few months after our detainment, the Engineer got a call from head office. 'We need people in the London office. We need you in two weeks' time. Are you in?'

London

CHAPTER 23

School and Snow

Yes, we were in. It was just before Christmas, but we were in.

We had visas to arrange, a house full of furniture, a cat and two pre-teen boys with the flu but I managed to get everything sorted out. Our shipment found its way to a warehouse. We put our cat on the plane and said goodbye to friends. Two weeks after the phone call, with visas in our passports, we disembarked at Heathrow airport.

In the first two weeks, Miguel, Isaak and I spent most of the day travelling up and down London on the underground, arranging schools and looking for a permanent home. Each day I saw signs of them adapting to the new culture.

'Hey, Manchester is playing Arse-hole this weekend.'

I felt the blood drain from my face as half the underground carriage laughed. The other half shuffled uncomfortably in their seats, knowing that you shouldn't lash out at a child. Eight-year-old Miguel sat unfazed, emulating the typical Englishman with his legs crossed and broadsheet newspaper in hand.

In their short lives, my boys had started and changed more schools than I had changed countries. I woke up with an ache in my jaw and a head full of fears for yet another first day at a new school. It was an underground ride and a twenty-five-minute walk from our temporary accommodation. In addition to this, I worried that the language switch would be a big stress. Although the school in Mexico had been bilingual, Isaak and Miguel had never had a full day of lessons in English.

So with a fair bit of trepidation, we started getting ready for English school. As I pulled back the curtains and looked out the window, I saw that the streets, the cars and the park benches were covered in snow. It rarely snows in London, so everything moved slowly that morning. It was the first time the boys had seen snow in the streets and it was a treat for all of us.

Miguel and Isaak's excitement took me back to my annual school athletics day in September 1981 in South Africa. Every kid had arrived at the athletics stadium wearing shorts. We had painted our faces with our house colours, but our arms and legs prickled with goose bumps. We had chanted our blue-lipped war cries with weak, vaporous voices. Some parents were huddled around an urn. When it was decided that it was too cold to run, we had been mercifully bussed back to school and, shivering and grumbling, went to our classes. But not even the teachers were in the mood for lessons. We were having a lukewarm discussion about nationhood when one of the jokers of the class, Shawn, always ready with a distraction, put up his hand. 'Miss? You teach geography. Do you think it will snow today?'

Mrs Geoteach, always looking for an opportunity to impart some knowledge, picked up a piece of chalk with her long delicate fingers and started explaining. 'As you all know, South Africa is very close to the Tropic of Capricorn, so the average temperature doesn't get very cold. This is just one of the reasons it doesn't snow here. We are close to 1,700 metres above sea level. This makes it very challenging for the conditions to be right for snow.' It had not snowed in Johannesburg for more than seventeen years. Mrs Geoteach continued her explanation about snow, but most of the kids had stopped listening. A few blank faces stared out the window. It wasn't too long before we were back in the realm of nationalism again.

For the second time, Shawn put up his chubby hand and asked about snow. Repressing her irritation with a deep breath, Mrs Geoteach explained snow again. This time most of us listened before returning to the original conversation that seemed to be getting further and further away.

When Shawn raised his hand for the third time, the entire class groaned. 'But, Miss, are you *sure* it won't snow today?'

Mrs Geoteach could no longer contain her sarcasm. 'I have explained to you why it will not snow. I have been a geography teacher for twenty-six years. Why exactly do you think that I don't know what I'm talking about?'

Shawn stood up with a big smile on his cheeky face. Slowly, he pointed out the window and said, 'It's not that I think you don't know what you are talking about, Miss. It's just, well, it's just that I think it *is* actually snowing.'

It was the first time I'd seen snow. It was one of the few times Johannesburg came together in the streets. Businessmen and women played alongside cleaners and labourers. Men, women and children of all colours, ages and races came together to throw snowballs at each other. It was the equaliser that gave people a taste of what life could be like in a colourless or rather, in the case of South Africa, a colourful rainbow nation.

I'd never forgotten that snow-filled magical school day when a boy asked a teacher, 'Miss, do you think it will snow today?' and it did.

The London snow removed the anxiety of starting a new school. Miguel and Isaak were cold and excited, and they couldn't wait to get to school to throw snowballs at kids their own age. Soon we were grappling with the new expectations of teachers and projects, but the gift of a snowy welcome brought hope for our new beginnings.

CHAPTER 24

Different Agendas

Like Spartans, my children were motherless from an early age. Unfed and poorly treated while in training, Spartans would punish hungry children not for stealing food, but for being caught. This taught them resilience.

Long before my children met me, they had learnt to be devious in order to survive. Sometimes they would combine forces and sneak up or swoop down on us. Other times they would choose to be centre stage, ensuring they got all the attention during an outburst. There were days the boys enjoyed contributing to the housework; other days they didn't.

One weekend the task of sweeping the small area in our entrance hall became the focal point of an argument with Miguel. Suddenly it was too hard, too unfair and too impossible. Eventually defeated, the Engineer said, 'Miguel, we're supposed to be at the park by now. I'm tired of waiting, and I'm tired of arguing. Give me the broom and I'll do it.' I thought it was a good solution but I was wrong. It turned out to be the catalyst for a longer, bigger and louder argument.

'No, I am *doing* it.' Miguel held on to the broom, his feet planted on the floor as though his life depended on it. He stared determinedly at the

Engineer, almost daring him to rip it out of his hands.

'But you are not doing it,' the Engineer said. 'Let me just do it so that we can – '

'No, I will do it.'

'Okay, do it so we – '

'No.'

'Then give me the broom.'

'I *said* I'm doing it.'

We could not think of any good way to end this argument. Our agendas were different. We wanted to leave the house and Miguel wanted to teach us a lesson.

Watching the Battle of the Broom, I realised that there was nothing the Engineer and I could do but wait for Miguel to change his mood.

Childhood games often prepare us for our future. As a child, I spent a lot of time by myself in our garden, meditating quietly before picking leaves and flowers for pretend potions. Being in touch with nature helped me in my adult life, but what would end up saving me was my other favourite pastime – that of being a 1970s KGB spy. As a pretend KGB agent, I came to understand the need for cunning. I tested myself by hiding tissues with words written on them, hoping to retrieve them later without detection. I would purposely bump my foot to become accustomed to pain. I taught myself to write with my left hand.

It might have been these KGB activities that got me through many a day with feisty Miguel and subdued Isaak. And like the KGB spy under deep cover, I felt that I could not explain my life to those around me. Only this time it wasn't a dirty tissue at stake; it was my children's lives and my sanity.

I had met Kim the first day I took the boys to their new school. She had seen me huddled in the cold, and taking pity on me, had invited me to wait with her in her car. Since then we had a weekly coffee date on a Wednesday, just before school came out. Today she seemed amused at my pain and I was starting to get irritated.

'This week, the boys sat for hours in one spot, refusing to study for their tests no matter how much I tried to help them. It's like they sabotage every opportunity we try to give them,' I said to her.

It often seemed that Miguel believed that if he waited a bit, everything would fall into place. That if he sat for three weeks doing nothing, his school project would magically be written up, or if he waited for five days, he would ace the English test. Or that if he covered his ears long enough to block out my voice, his maths exercises would miraculously be done.

'Once they fail, I'm sure they'll come around,' Kim told me. 'Kids don't like to fail.' Her naturally blonde hair and plain gold necklace glinted in the sun.

'But you see, they have been through so much more than failing a test that they don't follow the usual rules. Besides, it is not about the test. We want Miguel and Isaak to understand that if you want the gold star, you need to work for it. We are trying to teach the boys this bigger picture.'

Kim shrugged her shoulders. At times, I wondered if we should have let the boys fail. But we felt that, where possible, we should prevent any failures that would indicate they weren't good enough. We wanted to help Miguel and Isaak to achieve some, if not all, of their potential.

I could see I was not describing it well so when Kim asked about the most common arguments in my house, I chose the smallest things to share. Miguel was determined to retain his comfort zone in combat. Isaak took it all in, and then ignored me completely. Even though my children were small, Miguel's rage-filled force always threatened to overwhelm me, and at times Isaak's solitude froze me to my core.

'You can't brush my teeth, and you won't make me.'

'Why did you stop me from running across the road? I would have dodged the car. You don't know that I would not have.'

'You do my homework. I don't need to.'

'It's not my fault that I can't spell this word.'

'He did it.'

'I did it and you can't stop me.'

The arguments always bounced in a circular motion.

'My kids have said all of those things. It's just a kid thing. What do you expect?' Kim adjusted her chair and looked at me confrontationally. As I relayed these incidents, I was aware that my kids' behaviour seemed normal. It wasn't as if they suddenly started behaving like elephants. There are only so many ways a child can show rebellion; but in our case, it was always the *reasons* for the rebellion that tripped us up, and it all started with trust.

'There is a difference though,' I persisted. 'Your two little girls understand love. My children don't even trust me. How can I help them if they won't trust me?'

'My children often don't believe me either. So explain to me what's so different.' Kim smiled as if she'd caught me out.

The most basic of motherly instincts told me that I should be able to make my children feel safe. But the safer I made it, the higher they built the wall. Isaak didn't know he could trust himself, so how could he trust me? His processing had broken, and it seemed as if it might never fix itself. Miguel might never accept authority. He wouldn't even accept help. I felt that I was failing my children. Failing as a mother.

'Oh, Kim, I can't explain it,' I said with a sigh. 'We'll never even know some of the things my boys have been through. It's all so frustrating.'

Kim looked at me serenely and shook her head. 'Have you tried positive reinforcement? You just focus on what they are doing right and make sure they know about it.'

I wondered how I could clarify the situation to her. If we told Miguel that we were proud of him, he became defensive. It was as if the pressure to keep doing well was too much for him. Isaak, on the other hand, wanted to remain invisible. His monsters always lurked in the shadows. So if we praised him, he seemed to fear being noticed. It was an impossible conundrum. We didn't want to give him any reason to stay behind his curtain.

I slumped back in my seat. I didn't have the energy to tell Kim about the most recent misunderstanding. The memory of hair strewn on the black-and-white-checked tiles in the bathroom came to mind.

As a teenager, I would cut my long wild punky hair, even shaving odd areas or dyeing it with coloured streaks. I had no problem with my kids doing the same.

'Miguel, you are very good at cutting your hair,' I observed one day.

'Why do you always say I cut my hair? I don't,' he said, scowling at me.

'Miguel, there is no problem here. You did a good job. I've taken your brother to the barber twice since your last haircut. Are you telling me that Isaak is cutting your hair for you? That's also okay.'

'No. No one is cutting my hair. Why would I cut my hair and say I didn't?'

That was exactly what I was trying to work out.

'But, Miguel, I've just found the red paring knife in the bathroom with your hair on it. You were the only one who was in the bathroom, and your hair is all over the floor. You know, I can buy you the tools you need, if you want. I'm afraid you may cut yourself with the kitchen knife.'

'I DIDN'T CUT MY HAIR.'

'This is so unimportant. You don't need to feel scared.'

It took a few months before Miguel felt comfortable to acknowledge that he did sometimes cut his own hair. I could never understand why preserving this secret was so important to him. I couldn't comprehend how much control he demanded in his ten-year-old little life, but I began to realise that he felt he should not depend on anyone. A shared truth could bring about a certain degree of unwanted closeness. Even if it hurt him, he would not hand over control to anyone, least of all me.

The move to London had been relatively stress free, and the boys settled into a new life quickly. Still, struggles came in all forms and from everywhere. Well-meaning people offered advice which often left me feeling annihilated because they couldn't understand our situation. I did what I could to ensure that my boys were treated well or received the type of care other children got. Most of our clashes, however, took place in the inner sanctuary of our home. The Engineer and I were on a permanent war footing, which relentlessly chipped away at our souls as we fought side by side to love and protect our children. The more challenges we came across in life, the closer the Engineer and I got. Always pulling together and leaning on each other. It wasn't that we always agreed with each other, but we always found a way to look for common ground and a way to move forward as one. The lack of trust our children had towards us added another layer to the already complex role of parenting.

I'm sure it hurts all mums when a little one shouts, 'I hate you.' Yes, they are just words, but they cut deeply regardless of how thick-skinned you are. Having rescued our children from squalor and given them a softer future, our guilt at not getting it right was deep even without these painful words. Like a ninja, Miguel knew how to exploit my vulnerabilities in order to hurt me. How could he not? He had a master's degree in pain. He knew what buttons to push. He had learnt to resort to desperate measures in order to survive.

'Yesterday was not my friend and tomorrow may never come,' Miguel told me with certainty.

But for me, it was much more complicated.

Most kids will put up a fuss about things they don't want to do. For a child to accept or rebel against your authority, they must first concede that you are the one making the rules. This tacit understanding occurs in infancy, a stage our family had skipped. When kids grow up in an atmosphere of safety, they can explore their ideas and learn right from wrong; but if they don't buy into your influence, it makes nurturing unfathomable.

Ultimately, they will let you reward them or even take punishment from you because they trust you. Once the tantrums pass, they'll come for hugs and kisses. They accept that you know best. They accept that you are the parent. This basic parenting contract was never ours to enjoy.

In our case, no type of punishment or reward worked. What became clear to us was that both boys must have experienced life-and-death situations. Sometimes Miguel would accept our authority and sit on the 'naughty step', but if he chose to revert to his auto-protection mechanism, he would simply refuse. Frustratingly, there was nothing we could do about it because the only thing he feared was death itself, and it was the one thing he trusted we would not bring to him. Similarly, we couldn't use the reward system because when there is no trust in the next moment, there is no reason to believe that the reward will come.

Most kids enjoy a little cuddle, but not Miguel. The feel of human touch was too much for him. He didn't have a tantrum if you took his hand; that would have been easier to deal with. Instead, Miguel harboured secrets. It was very subtle, but if you watched, you would see it. The look he gave, the carefully disengaged moment when he judged you and then the very elusive unhanding. When I mentioned the tendency to my friends, they told me I didn't know him well enough. They thought I was just looking for problems. But the Engineer also picked it up and we were both mindful of it.

When we walked across the road, we were permitted to hold his sleeve, but not his hand. We realised this intimacy was something we couldn't rush. When your young child doesn't let you touch him, everything needs to be renegotiated. Bath time at this age is still a time for bonding. The warm water, the soft towel drying wet little bodies, all of it bringing intimacy and closeness. But this did not come naturally to our family. I was not a welcome presence in their bathroom.

With good intentions, we patiently waited and were eventually permitted to hold a hand now and then. With endurance, we could give Miguel a little hug while tucking him into bed. And finally, with persistence, we were allowed to give a kiss goodnight.

'Goodnight. Sleep tight. Let the faeries kiss.' Light hug, quick kiss.

You have no idea how much time it took and the fires that had to be extinguished before we could reach this point. Each time it happened I would take a deep breath in and hold on to that split second. I didn't want to let go, afraid that when I did, it would be the last time I would be allowed to touch him.

CHAPTER 25

Harry Potter and the Elusive Scones

We were living in the land of King Arthur, James Bond and Doctor Who, not to mention the most famous English kid in the world, Harry Potter. So how could we not take a trip to Hogwarts? It was surprisingly easy to get to. We didn't even have to run towards a wall on a station platform.

Hogwarts is known to muggles as Alnwick Castle, which is in the English countryside of Northumberland. There are about twenty-four castles in the area, and we made it our mission to see as many of them as possible. And then we made it our mission never to go looking for another English castle ever again.

While in the area, we found a camping ground where we chose to stay in a quaint and very warm wooden A-frame structure. Miguel and Isaak found some children the same age to play with, and for the first time in many years, the Engineer and I sat back and just watched the kids running around and having fun. At first, these blonde little English boys and girls didn't know what to make of our strange family dynamic, but once they ascertained that Miguel and Isaak spoke English and knew how to play cops and robbers, they didn't bother trying to work out who belonged where. They all just came together as one big precinct and ran around shooting the imaginary bad guys with plastic guns. At sunset, as if pre-arranged, the kids disbanded and hungrily went back to their families for food.

For the first time, it felt like we were a regular family. No emotional breakdowns. No hiding within myself. And no second-guessing our parental skills. Just a family unit exploring the English countryside. It gave us a break from the dysfunction of our lives and offered us hope that this might be our reset button.

The build-up to the holiday had been oppressive. Isaak had been trying to disappear into himself again and Miguel was once again trying to dominate his world.

The boys were allowed to use the new digital camera as long as they asked us first, and they usually did. One day I noticed the camera was out of its case. Miguel was standing in the doorway looking at me with a slightly challenging smile on his good-looking face. I felt the silence creep into the room as I looked at the last two pictures. Poor Isaak was sitting on the toilet, trying desperately to dodge the camera while not getting off the throne. The other was a faceless picture of Miguel standing in front of a mirror, camera lifted to his eye while the flash splashed its light on the silver surface.

I took a deep breath, looked at Miguel and could see that he was ready for me.

'Miguel, it's not nice to take a picture of someone on the toilet. It's a private place, and I can clearly see that Isaak didn't like you taking a picture of him.'

'I didn't take it. Isaak took it himself.' He threw the argument at me and waited for me to pick it up.

'You know I can't believe that. I can see Isaak sitting there with one hand pulling his pants up and the other hand stretched out towards you.'

'You never believe me,' he accused.

'Well, there are a few things going on here. I don't want you to take a picture of your brother on the toilet again. I also want to remind you of the house rule. You are supposed to ask before you use the camera.'

'It wasn't me, I tell you.'

'Miguel, describe the next photo to me in your own words, please.'

'I don't know. It's someone taking a picture of himself in the mirror. The flash is going off but you can't see his face.'

'So, you did take the picture then?'

'No, I DIDN'T. You can't prove anything.' He was still wearing the same sweater with the same dirty mark on the sleeve, and he was willing to admit that he was holding the camera. He confessed that the flash went off and he conceded that if the flash went off, a picture was being taken. But neither I nor any of the gods would get him to admit that he had taken the picture. In his mind, I couldn't prove anything.

'Look, I'm willing to overlook this because it's the first time it's happened. You don't have to worry, but I'd really like you to stop pretending that you didn't use the camera.'

'But it's not true. I didn't use the camera. I didn't take any pictures.'

Sitting on the deck of the A-frame, coffee in hand, watching the happiness unfolding around me, I could view the camera episode as a cute story about parenting. But at the time it was not just a story involving a camera, a child and his thinking. It was a scenario that repeatedly played out in the ongoing drama of managing our damaged child. I felt the sting of parental burnout. The Engineer and I often felt that it was never a question of winning or losing, just a question of how to manage to the best of our ability – and our ability never felt good enough.

We had a truce that holiday and the scarcity of English scones sent us on a unified mission as we drove around begging and pleading for scones at every teahouse and coffee place we could find. We were told that scones were out; panini sandwiches were in. On the last day, at the last place we went to, they found some frozen scones and reluctantly thawed them for us. In the end, it didn't matter that the scones were not fresh, we settled for them sitting on the table in front of us. Putting the whole picture together – castles, friends and scones – it was the best of times.

Driving home with cream and jam still sticky on our fingers, we all had smiles on our faces. On our way back to London that day, I felt we could conquer the world.

CHAPTER 26

A Cry for Help

The grey-haired lady walking towards me was struggling with her umbrella and trying to tame her handbag as her jacket hung limply from her hand. Her round shoulders suggested years of working at a desk. I was still wet from the summer London rain and I took pity on her as I noticed a look of harassment on her creased face.

'It's stopped raining now, no need to struggle with the umbrella,' I suggested.

She shot me an acerbic look. 'Oh, mind your own fucking business,' she mumbled as she tottered off, leaving me feeling relieved that I hadn't offered to carry her bag. I found myself laughing manically at my predicament. While I was simply trying to make her day easier, she aggressively put me in my place. I was out of my depth in the streets of London and at home too. But I didn't know how to stop trying to help people when I saw them struggling.

By now my days were filled with as many psychology books as I could find. I had a need to understand my world and the people I had brought into it. My strong relationship with the Engineer helped me get through some of the tougher days that were not only filled with the usual arguments that kids have with their parents, but also overflowed with the more complicated needs of our family. Whether he was at home or travelling on business, he was always able to hold me up when I thought I would fall apart. I had started to notice that my temper flared more quickly than usual. There were days when my whole body ached with the stress of holding myself together and trying to understand the reason why I could not find an opening to my sons' hearts. I had headaches. I began to find it difficult to concentrate. I longed to be able to go away on my own to sit quietly and stare into the nothingness, but in England, although I had some friends and a cousin who would often drop everything to listen to yet another teary conversation with a woman on the verge of a nervous breakdown, I felt very alone. I had lost interest in everything other than trying to fathom what I was dealing with and why my institutionalised kids couldn't trust those around them. While attempting to help others, I was losing myself.

And then another piece of the puzzle fell into place.

It was one of those rare London summer days when the sun came out and every man, woman and child, in fear of missing some blue sky and vitamin D, took to the streets. Miguel and Isaak had joined a family friend at the Natural History Museum. By the time we sat down around the kitchen table recounting the morning's outing, we thought the day's adventure was over. But it had only just begun.

Suddenly we heard the dry crackling sound of twigs and branches burning just beyond our garden. We ran to investigate, only to find a fire raging in the neighbouring yard as a result of an unattended barbeque. With the firemen dealing with a nearby timberyard fire, we had no choice but to act fast and put the garden fire out ourselves. Isaak jumped to attention and manned the taps while we poured buckets of water on the burning bushes. Once again, Isaak instinctually knew what to do in a time of danger. By now the Engineer and I recognised that the only time he became fully aware was when there was a threat. In contrast, we were surprised by Miguel's reaction. His aggression fled in the face of imminent danger. Glued to the spot in the middle of our garden as flames licked the fence, he didn't know what to do or where to hide. He was overwhelmed with the magnitude of the fire and for only the second time, I saw my angry boy simply freeze. I realised in life-threatening situations, Miguel felt out of control and was left without a response mechanism. No amount of psychology books and research could have explained my boys' inner worlds better than what I witnessed that day. If only I had understood better what I'd seen, maybe I could have used the information to help them heal from the trauma of their early lives.

School was never kind to me as a child. It turned out that it would not be kind to me as a parent either. But at school, if I failed a test, I knew that I hadn't done enough preparation. In the school of parenthood, however, I did what I could and more than I thought I was capable of. At times, I may have acted unconventionally and I was often misunderstood, but I believe I did what was necessary. But the most painful realisation was that my best parenting wasn't enough.

In our search for family peace, we were referred to a reputable institute in London that helped with family issues. The pros relished our unusual story of cross-cultural, older adoption with dysfunctional and highly problematic kids. We would meet every two weeks with our team of psychologists and social workers, and we would unburden ourselves of our troubles, fears and pain. But the Engineer and I were looking for answers and guidance, not simply a place to offload our stories. When we walked out of the office, we couldn't be sure that anyone had understood that we felt we were failing to help our children. They spoke to us with soft, comforting voices. And then the session was over.

We needed more.

I chose to end our journey with the institute during what turned out to be our last meeting with the therapist. It started with some misguided listening.

'Isaak feels comfortable with pain and we've noticed that he'll often put himself in harm's way,' I said. 'Do you think it's because he knows danger better than safety and so he goes to the familiar?'

'What do you mean? Can you give me an example?' the therapist asked.

'He somehow finds his finger caught in the door or scrapes his knee where it is almost impossible to get scraped. The other day he shmooshed his little face between the swings.'

'Is he doing it on purpose?' she asked, gazing at the fish tank.

'Yes. He even goes so far as to put his hand somewhere that it's sure to get hurt. I *see* him doing it.'

'How long has he been self-harming?' the therapist asked, leaning forward and starting to scrummage around in her bag for something to write on. It seemed I'd suddenly piqued her interest.

'No, no, he isn't self-harming,' I said. 'This is different. He is just running towards the damage.'

It wasn't the first time there had been a misunderstanding in our communication about our children. I had been to lectures and spoken to parents whose kids self-harmed; their plight seemed different from ours. I wanted desperately for the therapist to understand what I meant.

'Many kids who come from difficult situations will self-harm,' the therapist told me. 'They feel numb and pain gives them a release of some sort. I didn't realise Isaak was doing that.'

'He is not self-harming,' I insisted. 'He is putting himself in harm's way. A hand purposely in the door. A foot intentionally placed where it will get stood on. In times of danger, he knows what to do. But when it's calm, there is a problem. I don't think it's the same thing.'

'It isn't anything you are doing wrong,' she assured me. 'Your situation is very hard.'

Although she was being supportive, I felt she was stuck on a misconception. I knew this wouldn't be the last time I would be misunderstood. I felt as though the Engineer and I were speaking a different language to the therapist. We had been seeing her for almost a year. We sometimes felt like she was collecting our interesting stories to use as research for a thesis or book.

In absolute desperation, I said, 'Look, we feel that we are not getting anywhere just talking. You guys have a lot of experience and we are looking to you for guidance. There must be something more we can do than just come here and talk about the fact that we're all struggling. There must be some advice you can offer us, some tools you can give us.'

The Engineer and I were familiar with why it was difficult and that we were 'handling it well', but I needed more than my ego stroked. Unfortunately for Isaak, and fortunately for the rest of us, life is not a series of dangerous situations. Now that he was in a safe place, his catatonic tics often re-emerged for no valid reason. He would still swing wildly in behaviour from being three years below his age group to three years above. Sometimes we felt he was on the autism spectrum, and on other days we couldn't fathom why we had thought such a thing. We were running out of ideas and we were drowning.

'You are doing a good job,' said the therapist. It was useless and invalid, and it took all my strength not to run out of her office. 'You know this is not a quick-fix situation. This is a long process and we can go in any direction you choose.'

Desperate and lost, I sobbed, 'I don't *know* where to go. If I knew, I wouldn't need permission to go there. I've done all the research I can. I've run my gut feelings into the ground and now, for all my intuition and investigating, we need help. Our boys need help.'

'We'll follow your lead and help you in any way you feel we can.'

I was begging for help, but it felt like the therapist was telling me that she would prefer to mind her 'own fucking business' – as though it wasn't her place to provide the tools I needed to help my children stand firm in life. I desperately wanted someone to say, 'Do this. Try that.' But all I was getting was, 'Very well done. Keep it up. Let us know what we can do.' There, in that stuffy office with a dirty blue carpet and calming fish tank, I felt that I was in a bizarre world, with no escape. I couldn't help feeling angry and frustrated. I had been living in hope that one day our family would have a moment of peace, but I was beginning to realise that was a myth. I still had fantasies of helping my children live happy and fulfilling lives but, at this point, I was no longer fooling myself about the reality of what was going on in our family dynamic. I went looking for coping strategies but to my despair, all I found was people telling me that I was doing well when I could see the beginning of my own unravelling.

On the subway going home, thinking of the fires I had put out for my boys and knowing about all the fires that were still rampant, I could hear a long and loud scream in my head. And it wouldn't stop. It was primal and fearful. It felt like the scream I would expect to hear at the end of days.

CHAPTER 27

The Unwanted

As a child, I felt unwanted when I moved with my family to a new town. Mrs K, with her horn-rimmed glasses and flat voice, told my mother that the nursery school simply had no space for me. The town was new for me, but it wasn't new for my family. I had lived there as an infant, but for my five-year-old self, it was not a homecoming. It was new and I already didn't like it. I had left my friends and everything that was familiar to me behind. Here in this old new town, I wasn't wanted. The nursery school was full.

My father's hardware store became my day-care centre for a while. By the time I started big school, I was tested with puzzles and children's stories, and I was found flawed. My skills in that area were lacking and I didn't know all the nursery rhymes. But I knew other things. I knew about product placement and marketing. I learnt to assess customers and developed a sensitivity to people's needs. I think my love for psychology began in the playground of the hardware store. That was where I gained an understanding of human nature and learnt to interpret the fact that sometimes a person might be in a bad mood simply because they didn't know how to fix their broken porch step.

When my mother received a call to say that the nursery school had found a way of accepting me, I was elated. I looked up at my mommy with my big green eyes and worshipped her achievement.

As a mother, I found myself on the flip side of the same story. In England, at the end of primary school, children sit an exam; the results of which determine the high school your child will attend. The Engineer and I were aware of how life changing this could be, so the exam became our focus.

Miguel and Isaak, by contrast, refused to do any preparation. We tried to help them understand what lay ahead but they would not budge. They sabotaged our every endeavour to support them.

One day after school Miguel's teacher came running out to talk to me at the gate. 'Miguel implausibly believes that he'll be able to pull the rabbit out of the hat,' she said to me, talking quickly and gesturing broadly. I knew that Miguel's superpower was rage combined with stubbornness. That week Miguel had sat for over three hours refusing to learn for the English preparation test. Everyone's nerves were frazzled. He steadfastly held his line, even if it meant sacrificing his free time.

'I know what you are saying, but I don't know how to fix it. I keep trying but he will not do any work he doesn't feel like doing. And to make matters worse, Isaak follows everything his brother does so neither of them are working.' I was conscious of the wild movements I was making with my hands.

'Miguel believes that if he just waits, he'll know how to do something. Or he'll ace the test. No amount of logic persuades him otherwise,' his teacher said. Her words echoed my daily fears for my son's future.

'Yes. He just thinks life will take the route he has determined it should. Once he makes up his mind about something, he doesn't let reality get in his way. It's not easy dealing with a child's magical thinking.' I felt like a schoolgirl gossiping about the naughty kid in the corner.

'He doesn't like doing something if he doesn't know how to do it, but in class, I've been trying to teach the kids that with practice, they will be able to master things. He just doesn't seem to get it. I feel like I am failing him,' she said with a worried look on her face. I knew that feeling all too well. I felt it on a regular basis.

We didn't want to stress Miguel and Isaak, but we were very concerned about their choice to do nothing. Try as we might, the boys slithered and slipped out of any work that would have made the exam easier for them. When exam week came, we knew we'd be in a war zone but nothing forewarned us of the backlash that came with the boys' failure to prepare. Miguel was a whirlwind of destruction. He believed everything was my fault and shot a barrage of rebellion my way. I was getting tired of hearing, 'I'm not doing it.' No matter what the 'it' was. Even fun was rejected simply because it was my suggestion. Sleep, eat, play, everything became a negation with Miguel attempting to dominate all decisions. He obstinately changed his opinion based on my reaction at every turn, even to his own detriment. It was just important to him that he take the opposing view.

Isaak, on the other hand, withdrew to the land of dreams where he felt safe and wouldn't emerge or awaken to life. I was forced to revert to old and cruel tricks to get him to start feeling again. There was no time for me to feel despairing or incapacitated. My job was to get everyone feeling strong and motivated.

Weeks later, we received the expected results. The school of our choice – one that was run with meticulous precision and offered the kinds of support our boys needed – did not offer places to our sons.

It was accepted wisdom that once you'd received a letter denying your child access, the school board was highly unlikely to change their mind. But I was determined to get my boys what they needed. Now I had to fight for my children's placement just like my mother had done for me all those years ago. I realised that in the end, all it had taken was a mother's perspective. As usual, the Engineer and I tackled the problem as a team. I wrote letters pleading for an audience with the school board and the Engineer edited them. We researched any possibility that might shift their mindset. Many times people reminded me of the unlikelihood of our success; nevertheless, I wrote and rewrote letters and wouldn't stop until we were given an audience. I am usually a shy person and generally lack confidence in the face of authority. I certainly wouldn't have put in such an effort for myself. But I was a mother now and I became ferocious. I evoked the lion and the bear and all the spirit animals I could muster to make sure that these two little people could get the support they needed.

Eventually, we were granted an audience with the school board: one forty-five-minute appointment. We brought in every bit of weaponry we had, plus a few harps and heartstrings. In our pleading, we exposed our full story to the strangers sitting around the boardroom table.

'We understand that it isn't the school's responsibility to look after every child who has had a tough time, but we were hoping for a little bit of leniency,' the Engineer began. 'Although English is our home language, it is not our children's first language. They arrived here mid-year and due to their age were forced to start a year above the level they'd been in so they were not ready for the level of exam that they wrote.'

I sat next to him nervously fidgeting with my hair. 'Also,' I interrupted, 'in an added twist of fate, they know enough English to not to be considered foreign. This meant that they weren't able to have an aid in the exam, which is what other kids who don't speak English were eligible for. All this added to a low mark on their exam.' I was trying not to be pushy, but I wanted the board to understand the full situation.

'Every one of our children's friends has been accepted into this school,' the Engineer continued. 'From early on in their lives, our boys have known rejection and we worry about yet another implied rejection for them.'

This school had a very good reputation for their special-needs department. We understood the impact that would have on the nuanced requirements our children had. Where most parents would have one reason why their kids should go to this school, we came with every angle of argument. When we walked out of that meeting, we weren't feeling confident, but we knew we had done everything possible. Then we returned home and tried to avoid the guerrilla warfare which had never subsided. We came to understand that any new bump in our daily lives would only give an excuse for a new argument. It would not add a new tension, only provide a focus for the one that was already there. It all boiled down to three simple truths: lack of trust, keeping us at bay and never learning to attach.

Although Miguel and Isaak were upset that they hadn't done well enough to get into the same school as their friends, like most kids that age, they didn't know the decision could be reversed. To them, we were the representatives of the adult world that was blocking their chosen path. They didn't recognise the school as the obstacle – we were the face of their exclusion. We were the ones telling them they couldn't go where their friends were going, and so their anger and disappointment were directed at us. Miguel and Isaak were scared to hope for the best. As we had feared, they interpreted their rejection from the school as just another proof that they didn't deserve what their friends did.

For three weeks we waited. For three weeks we wondered. And for three weeks we ducked and dived the anger and the silence until the deadline arrived. We opened the letter. It was hard to believe it but we had actually pulled it off. The Engineer and I were elated. We couldn't wait to share the good news with Miguel and Isaak. But when we did, they simply shrugged and walked off. I know the psychology of it – they couldn't bring themselves to show us that they were happy to get what they had wanted – but still, it hurt.

We made history that year. I experienced the same relief I'd felt as a child when I was accepted into the nursery school. From now on it would be the school that would have it all under control. I was elated. I revelled in this hard-won victory. We had done it for our boys. And I mistakenly thought I would never have to do school homework again.

CHAPTER 28

Trains, Planes and Automobiles

When I was single, travel was my demon and my angel. My personal seraph coaxing me on, telling me where to go and what to do. I never used a guidebook. I would just step into an unknown street, choose a direction and pick a person to follow.

Once, a girl with dreadlocks walked past me down a Scottish street. She was humming to herself and didn't notice me inconspicuously step out and trail her. I remember pulling my knitted sweater closer to me in a battle against the wind. This girl was almost skipping and then I heard a rhythm floating in the air. A drumbeat. She started to skip faster and then she began to run. I remember running too. I was running fast by the time I passed her. She looked at me knowingly. We were both running to the rhythm. It guided us around the corner and at the same time, as if one, our thoughts interrupted, we couldn't help ourselves, our face muscles shifted into smiles. We had come across an impromptu music festival. I think it took her as much by surprise as it did me. Each of us was transported back to places we'd been before. There was no time to talk. There was no time to think. We just started dancing. I danced into the night. This experience was not something a guidebook could ever give me.

The next day I found myself following another unknown leader as I wandered down a dusty pathway wearing a flowing skirt and flimsy shoes. He led me to a river and as he crossed through it, I had to know where he was going. Then slowly, ever so slowly, my foot gave way. My body followed the gravitational pull while my skirt did not. I ended up in the cold water with my skirt above my head. So much for discretion. I heard wolf whistles, catcalls and clapping. I have always known when it is time to move on.

By ten, the boys were adept travellers and I thought it was the perfect time to share my passion for travelling with them. I invented a game that we played in airports and underground stations. They would lead the Engineer and me all the way onto the plane, train or bus. They learnt to fill out airport forms and judge the best route to take when we were on undergrounds. They were naturals, and because it gave them a defined amount of control, there would be a peace accord whenever we played the game.

In the summer holidays, the boys took us from London by train to France and Spain. In Paris, we went to the Louvre, ate lots of crêpes and baguettes, and walked along the Champs-Elysées. In Barcelona, we visited Gaudi's buildings, ate lots of tapas and paella, and wandered down the streets of the Gothic Quarter. And then we flew to Morocco.

The trip was a mingle of days of tranquillity and evenings of arguments with Miguel while Isaak ignored us and did his own thing. He would disregard any family rules or connections.

'Isaak, I see you are looking at the cute kitten. Remember, don't play with it. It looks like it's a bit wild and we don't know it. It might carry diseases,' the Engineer reminded him as we walked from our room to the lunch table.

'Yes, I know. It can scratch me,' Isaak responded, looking at the ginger kitten longingly. Moments later we heard a sharp intake of breath and turned around to see Isaak trying to hide his hand from us.

'What happened, Isaak?' I asked, almost knowing the answer before he gave it.

'The tiny cat scratched me,' Isaak said, looking up at me with a smile on his face. 'I leaned down to pat it and I think I scared it,' he added, not wanting to get the cat into trouble.

'But we just told you not to play with the cat,' the Engineer said, a bit dumbfounded.

'Yeah, I forgot.'

It wasn't the first time and it wouldn't be the last that we were disregarded. There was no point in arguing, so we went in search of something to clean the bleeding scratch. Sometimes we would ask Isaak not to wander off and then we find him on his own somewhere. We knew to expect the unexpected with him.

No *one* disagreement was different from any other parents arguing with their children, but the decisiveness and refusal to accept our well-meaning direction was sucking at my core. Our arguments never moved on or progressed, and I still didn't know how to deal with them. We fought over everything and anything. Our authority meant nothing to the boys and it usually made holidays difficult because I never had a moment to recoup. I never had those soft little reprieves when a child snuggled up to me or looked to me for affection. At every turn I was trying to work out what would come next, why it was happening and what the best way to do any number of things was without the extra layer of dis-ease that was rooted in the time before I knew my children.

But it was while we were travelling in Morocco, with its layers of complexity and exceedingly kind local people, that a fleeting change came about. Whether it was against the backdrop of the terracotta sunset, or in the richly coloured market filled with ancient snake charmers and offerings of green mint tea, or the mosaic-tiled beauty of the opulent palaces, but wherever we went, the boys received gifts and treats. It made them forget themselves for a while. This country spoke to them, something raw and real whispered to them.

Morocco is not a soft place. There are hardships and hunger, and waves of extreme transformation. It made the boys pause and assess where they were in life, and where they might have ended up. Seeing small kids working hard and eking out a living in the market stalls provided a sharp contrast to our lives. While these children worked, we arrived in an air-conditioned taxi with bottled water. The experience had a profound effect on all of us. I think these images and feelings made their way into the boys' subconscious, letting them know that they were lucky enough to be given some opportunities that these street urchins were not. An unseen chance at a life of comfort and care.

We stayed at a riad, where Mehdi, the owner's son, took us to local markets where people stood to the side and watched the only tourists in the place buy a tajin. He led us up a mountain where we sat on plastic chairs and ate the cuisine of the area with his friends. He also taught the boys archery.

The trip was a great success, but as I sat in the plane on the London tarmac waiting to disembark, the familiar feeling of unease crept in. I had become conditioned into expecting tantrums after fun and I held my breath in trepidation.

There was no immediate tantrum. Not a word or a look or even a huff. Just quiet contentment. I was fearful that this win would not last long, but I took it. I sat there feeling my victory, almost too scared to move lest it slip from my grasp.

Of course, by the next week, old habits returned. Miguel continued to look for an argument, stubbornly ignoring every request and house rule. In short, he lived by his own rules and fought for control of everything he did regardless of whether it was for his own good or not. Isaak continued to keep me at bay. He ignored me and the house rules. This included his own health and hygiene. Both boys distorted the truth at every turn, even when they didn't need to. I continued reading as much as I could in the hope of finding a way to bond with our children. I attempted to let them learn their own lessons, but sometimes, taking this approach felt like saying to a small child, 'Okay, run into the road if you want to. Let's see how that works out for you. If it turns out badly, then we'll see how we might better manage it next time.'

Sometimes I just needed to take a deep breath and yell, 'STOP,' as loudly as I could because children are just children and they don't know better. But *I* did know better. And things *were* going badly. My pain was turning me into a closet shut-in.

'I'm meeting your cousin for coffee. Why don't you join us? We haven't seen you for so long,' Kim said from the other end of the phone. I had cancelled on her three times and I wondered why she still tried to get me out of the house.

'I'd love to, Kim, but I am really busy at the moment,' I lied. I just couldn't face opening up to her anymore.

'Look, I know you were having headaches the last time we were going to meet, and the time before you were exhausted and needed an early night, but you need to get out and have a little bit of fun. Please just meet us for a coffee,' she implored.

'Okay, Kim, I'll be there. But no more questions about how things are going at home. We're fine now.' Even I could hear the insincerity in my voice, but I didn't have the energy to talk about anything other than the mundane.

'Are you and the Engineer okay?' she continued, disregarding my request. Kim knew that he was on a business trip and she always assumed that I felt alone. I was never able to explain to her that even if he was not in the country with me, we handled everything together.

'Yes, Kim, we are fine. He is always supportive. When things are going wrong with the boys, it doesn't matter where he is – he stops everything to support us. We are stronger than most couples who are never apart.'

'Well, that's good to hear,' she said, her voice thick with disbelief. I could see why she didn't understand. The Engineer and I were unconventional in the way we dealt with our lives. In any type of adversity, we pulled together. Our strengths complemented each other and because of that, we were always strong. We would laugh and joke with each other as if we were teenagers, and there wasn't anything we wouldn't do for each other.

'You know, you don't have to keep things to yourself. You have friends to talk to. I think sometimes you expect a little bit too much from your children and it makes your life harder,' Kim continued.

'That is so kind of you to say and I know I can talk to you. It's just that sometimes it's hard to put it into words. The boys have been through things that were extreme. Sitting in this first-world country, people often underestimate the squalor that can go on in an orphanage. After all this time, adjusting into family life is still hard for them.' I tried to explain it one last time. 'Don't worry about me. I'm fine, the boys are fine, everything is good, and I'll see you for coffee with painted lips and all,' I said with a smile in my voice. I already knew that I would cancel at the last minute. There just wasn't a way to explain why our problems, which seemed so tedious to Kim, went deeper. It wasn't that any one thing that happened in our house was different in a hundred other houses, but put together and on top of each other, it was relentless.

I had to remind myself that life is just life and there was nothing to do but plod along its path, regardless of how it was playing with me. If Struggle drops in for tea, we don't have the option of throwing him out. He just sits himself down and enjoys the last of the homemade scones.

I had to learn to take the bad with the bad.

I took strength in knowing that I was finding some tools to give to my children, even if they were wrapped in travel trips. I just put a brave smile on my face and I went out into the world like the big girl I was pretending to be.

CHAPTER 29

London's Burning

> SMS to the Engineer:
>
> MIRIAM'S HOUSE IS ON FIRE

When I was a child, in between my pretend KGB training and my young witch's potions, I invoked spells at the bottom of our garden where no one could see me. They were usually failed attempts at hindering my school bullies: *Please make Dan stop picking on me. Tomorrow Sarah will not tease me about my big ears.* But the magic words scrawled on a paper and burnt with a match never worked. As a naive child playing with fire, of course I had no idea that I'd be putting out fires for the rest of my adult life.

One fine English-winter's day, when the Engineer was on a business trip in Sweden, I had a witchy feeling. The whole week I had felt uneasy about something and I couldn't explain why. It wasn't because the Engineer was away. He had always travelled. The feeling of unease continued for the whole week.

> SMS to the Engineer:
>
> OUR HOUSE IS ALSO ON FIRE

The school day usually ended at 3pm, but that niggly Friday the boys were going to the library, so I only had to pick them up at 4pm. As the day wore on, my edgy feeling heightened. It was 2:40 but I decided to leave early and find something to do near the school until it was time to collect them.

As I walked down our garden path, I looked at the pretty rosebushes in bloom but what I smelt was the acrid fumes of burning rubber strips wafting from the tradesman on our neighbour's roof. He was fixing the waterproofing. Our neighbours had lived in the adjoining semi-detached house for twenty or thirty years. They had been through the trials and tribulations that come with bringing up five children. When we first moved in, Miriam was there to offer whatever help we needed.

I ambled along the pathway to my car and looked at my watch again. As I drove off, I knew that I would have a long wait at the school. It turned out the wait didn't take that long.

'Hey, we don't need to go to the library anymore,' Miguel said over the phone. 'Isaak and I did the work during lunch. Can you pick us up now?' He sounded tired. The night before he had snuck downstairs to watch TV in the middle of the night and hadn't slept much.

'Are you sure? You guys don't usually like to work during the lunch break.' I had just pulled up outside the school.

'Nah, we're done.'

> SMS to the Engineer:
>
> I LEFT THE BOYS AT LARA

I didn't want another argument with the boys, so we drove home listening to music, each of us lost in our own thoughts.

'I think a house is on fire,' Isaak said, pointing to the smoke in the sky as we rounded the corner into our street.

'No, sweetie, I think it is a low cloud,' I assured him. My premonition took a back seat for the first time that week. Life had been a bit of a rollercoaster lately, and I just wanted things to be simple, even if it was just for a few more minutes.

'No, I think it is a fire.' Isaak was wearing his alert face.

Halfway down our street, flames were reaching up to the sky. *Our house was halfway down the street.* I could no longer ignore what I already knew.

In life's helter-skelter moments, I become focused. There was no more denying it: things were definitely not going to be simple that day.

> SMS to the Engineer:
>
> CAT'S STUCK IN THE HOUSE

A high-pitched scream was coming from the middle of the road. As I turned my head to my burning house, I realised it was coming from Miriam. Her memories were busy burning in the house while she stood helplessly looking on in the middle of the road and wailed. One of her daughters was there shouting into the phone: 'Well, where the fuck is the fire engine? We called what seemed like ages ago. Now we've got *two* houses on fire and you guys are having bloody *tea*.'

Men and women stood around not knowing what to do while Miriam continued to scream. I took it all in as we ran past, slowing down to give her a quick hug of support and to ask if anyone was inside her house.

SMS to the Engineer:

IT'S STARTING TO RAIN.
THE FIREMEN JUST ARRIVED.

I didn't want my kids to watch our house with our belongings and our beloved Mexican cat, Cazadora, go up in smoke. I took them to my friend Lara, whose house was on the next street. I was relieved to see her blue car parked outside her cute, little white semi. I put my finger on the door buzzer and didn't take it off until the door opened.

'Can't talk, house on fire.' I saw the look of bewilderment on her face as I shoved the kids into her house and bolted.

Back at my house, all I could think of was our beloved cat who was locked inside. I was not about to lose her to a stupid house fire. As I reached the door of our flaming house, I put the key in the lock. A homeowner in the street came out of nowhere, grabbed me and physically moved my body away. Legs and arms flying, I shouted every obscene word I could think of. I wanted to give my cat an option of running out, but this neighbour was determined to save me from an imminent gas explosion. Every time I took a step towards the door, he moved me like I was a piece of garden furniture.

'Look, you have a choice,' I finally said to him. 'Either you can stand here arguing and moving me, and maybe get blown up trying to stop me, or you can let me open the goddamn door.'

He relented, and just as I opened the door, the firemen arrived. By this time our roof was fully ablaze. With extraordinary speed and efficiency, the firemen ran into our house and up the stairs. They fought the fire from the inside of our ceiling. A burly fireman spread plastic protective sheets over my furniture, saving our possessions from water damage.

SMS to the Engineer:

MIRIAM'S HOUSE BURNED DOWN.
WE FOUND THE CAT.
WE'LL BE AT THE HOLIDAY INN TONIGHT.

It was obvious that Miriam's house was lost, but they did their best to save what they could. All I could do was stand in the street holding her hand. She was now standing quietly with her daughters, an empty look on her face. We held on to each other while a frenzied version of the song 'Burning Down the House' played repetitively in my head.

SMS from the Engineer:

JUST FINISHED A LOOONG MEETING.
I DON'T GET YOUR JOKE.

When we were allowed back in the house, we found it waterlogged, the electricity was dodgy, the roof had a hole in it and our clothes were smoke-damaged. We'd lived in that London house for two years. We were all fine, our things were fine, our cat was fine, but we could no longer live there. It was time to move.

Three weeks after the fire the Engineer got another call from head office. 'We need people in Sydney and Melbourne: you choose which you want. Are you in or are you out?'

Sydney

CHAPTER 30
Living with Family

My mother and my sisters' families had ended up living in Sydney. Were we in or were we out? We were in, of course. I started to imagine having the support which, until then, had eluded me. Family. Every kid should have aunts, uncles, cousins and grandparents nearby. In Sydney, our boys would have it all. All except the exceptional school we had fought so hard to get them into.

We thought about this move more carefully. Even as a child, I had always been in love with London and its location in the world. To me, Sydney seemed to be at the bottom of the planet. We balanced the advantage of proximity to family for the kids and the disruption of an extra move, an extra school and new friends against what we had in London. When we looked at the whole picture, the benefits of moving our children outweighed the costs. The access to extended family was pivotal. We packed our bags and headed Down Under. Ugg boots and Aussie Rules, here we come.

Although the Engineer had a month to finish his projects and the Australian school year was starting in four weeks, we decided it would be a good idea to go early so that the boys could make friends before starting at a new school. The rush was on to clean our waterlogged, smoked-enveloped clothes and get our shipment of goods quoted, packed and moved, along with our beautiful cat who had made it through the fire adventure unscathed. We said goodbye to the school and the friends we had made along the way. We did everything calmly and it went smoothly.

I am an excellent mover. They say moving is one of the most difficult things one can do, but this is not true for me. I have become an expert mover of homes and because I am an introvert, I find it easier than asking a friend to the movies.

Within two weeks the boys and I got on a plane and headed towards the rest of our family. Miguel and Isaak would learn *Advance Australia Fair* and forget about saving the Queen. When we moved from Mexico to England, the boys had skipped a grade at school, which I had never felt good about. In London, they were already in high school and we were losing the war against time. In Sydney, they'd be eleven-year-olds back in middle school. We would gain back a year, which would help while we tried to catch up some development progressions. It all lined up well. They would even have the bonus of being slightly ahead in maths. The ethos of all the schools we'd chosen around the world was similar, so we were not too worried about the boys fitting in. To make it even easier, their cousins attended the same school they'd be going to.

Within the first two weeks of arriving in Sydney, Miguel and Isaak met some schoolkids on the beach and by the time the first day arrived they were feeling confident.

We stayed at my sister's house until we found a place of our own. We had intended to move to Maroubra, famous for its waves and infamous for a surfer-dude gang known as the Bra Boys. Housing in Maroubra was a little closer to our budget but a little further from the rest of my family. In the end, we landed up living closer to our family and a little bit further away from our original budget.

When it comes to barbeque, sports and sunshine, the suburbs of Sydney are very similar to those of Johannesburg. With the influx of South Africans in the '80s and '90s, even the accents have melded together. Swap a Black Label for some Four X beer, call a braai a barbie and no worries, mate, she'll be right.

It turns out that it's easier to move to a place that is completely different to your culture than to relocate to one that is similar. I'd adapted to different cultures, countries and customs, become used to strange and wonderful new things and even learnt different languages, but the fact is that similar is just not the same.

I had left home at seventeen. My mother and sisters still saw me as that scrawny teenager even though I was now a middle-aged mother of two. I had lived successfully in five other countries and yet I was being taught how to catch a bus. My mother would introduce me to her friends saying, 'And this is my baby.' I would follow their gaze to the smallest of us standing next to her and they would smile, slightly bewildered, at the little brown boy with black hair and dark eyes. I could see the confusion on their faces. I'd wait a couple of seconds before explaining in the clearest way possible, 'No, I'm the baby to whom my mother is referring. The little boy is mine.' Confusion would abound over the clearly cross-cultural family with different skin tones.

My two sisters are dynamic women. They are quick learners, and teachers often made the mistake of thinking I'd be the same. But it became clear that not only was I not on the 'same page' as them, I was often not reading the same book. If the topic was the sun, for example, they'd be talking about global warming while I'd be contemplating how warmly to dress that day. Growing up, I idolised them in different ways. I wanted their approval, but as younger sisters often do, at times I got in their way. I would want to play while they needed to study.

My eldest sister had always made me feel protected and cared for. She had taught me how to cook when I was a little girl. She had spoken to my schoolteacher when things were going wrong and she had shown me how to shave my legs. My middle sister had tried to teach me how to grow up. Before I went to school, she attempted to teach me how to read, she showed me how to add sums and, a little unwillingly, allowed me to copy her handwriting style. But my sisters approached life from a different angle to me. Now I was all grown up. I had found my own identity and yet I was still the youngest sibling. I didn't know how to let my sisters and mother know that I was an adult now. How do you tell a person who loves you that you are an adult and no longer need their protection? Or that the lessons you've learnt are different from what they thought you would need?

My transition into Sydney was thus quite challenging. My family tried very hard to 'settle me in'. So hard, in fact, that I felt robbed of the little authority I had over my children. In their determination to help me, there were times when I found they didn't always understand the type of assistance I needed and often, more importantly, why I needed to be the type of parent I had become. Miguel and Isaak started seeing me as the little sister rather than the mother I was trying to be. I began questioning my capabilities. The people around me left me feeling invisible.

Even though I had left Mexico two years before, it was in Sydney with all its South Africans that I felt I stood out. In London, we were just another immigrant family; but in Sydney, I didn't fit in well with the Joburg expats and I wasn't recognised by the locals either. I found myself having conversations about the bad postal system, and health and safety issues I knew and cared nothing about. The Engineer and I did not easily assimilate into our beautifully safe neighbourhood with its friendly people with whom I had very little in common.

I missed Mexico more than ever before. When I first moved there, I nearly fainted in a man's shop. He insisted that I sit down while he left his shop with me in it. He returned with a chocolate bar and a drink, and he made me stay until he thought the colour had returned to my face. A few days later, he saw me on the street and approached to ask how I was feeling. I noticed the difference when one day, in Sydney, I tripped and fell in the street. As I lay sprawled on the pavement, people politely stepped around me. Nobody bothered to check why I was on the ground. I longed for the comfort of strangers.

In Mexico, my visa did not permit me to work; and in England, the

Engineer's company had paid for most of our ongoing living expenses. The move to Australia did not come with the same perks. I needed to find work but I was no longer on a career path. My choices had dwindled with each move we made; nevertheless, I was lucky enough to find a job in customer service and admin. It was a full-time job with an early shift, which meant if I rushed, I could be home just before the kids got back from school. The benefit of this was double-edged. While I could be there to help make sure their homework got done, this meant that I remained their unwelcome taskmaster. While I was trying to show my family that I had grown up, and I was a mother and the Engineer was a father, we slowly settled back into our typical family routine.

School during the week, sport during the weekend and therapy when needed. We had grandmother lunches and aunts and uncles and cousins coming and going. The boys started school without a hitch initially, and I remember thinking we were finally on a good road. We started to preen and boast that we had at last started living a 'normal' life. And at that point, Murphy called up Confucius and said, 'Get a load of these people. We must do something about it. I feel we've been remiss.'

CHAPTER 31

Jekyll and Hyde

There were days when I thought I was insane. I would walk out of the house and see a dark cloud hovering above me. Isaak would be zombie-ing and Miguel would be raging. I was presented with only two states of being: solitude and rage. We would walk in silence to the car, sit in our self-inflicted exiles from each other and drive off. When the car came to a stop and we joined the rest of the human race at a soccer game or family dinner, out popped two helpful, kind, well-mannered and vocal boys. Friendly, loveable and willing to extend a gentle hand to anyone who needed it. Soft faces, soft eyes and soft voices. I would look at them in bewilderment and feel like I'd lost my grip on reality. The Engineer too, felt unmoored. Our alternate realities were unsettling. A few minutes ago, we were in a state of havoc with the hellhounds released, but now the boys were generous, loving and appreciative.

'You are so lucky to have such wonderful boys.'

'Your boys are so well mannered and softly spoken.'

'I wish my kids were so helpful around the house.'

I would hear such praise from strangers, friends and family alike.

How could I explain our Jekyll and Hyde existence? The truth is our boys *did* demonstrate the qualities others attributed to them. They just didn't show them to the Engineer or to me. Some of my friends and family would shake their heads and tell me I expected too much. That my sons were loving and caring, and I should count myself lucky. I suspected they thought I was lying when I tried to give them an inkling of the dynamics at home.

One day Isaak told my mother that his bed was broken, which was the reason he hadn't been sleeping well. Being a caring grandmother, she called us to find out why we had not fixed the bed. The Engineer and I were very confused because two years previously, we had bought Isaak a very comfortable, brand-new bed. Since then, we hadn't noticed any issues and Isaak hadn't reported any problems. When we checked the bed, we found it was still fine. We asked Isaak about it.

'The bed is good. It's comfortable,' he said.

'But then why did you say that you aren't sleeping because the bed is broken?'

'I dunno. Isn't it broken?' He said this as if it was a new conversation unrelated to the previous question about the bed.

'Don't you remember that when your old bed was breaking, we bought the new one that you're sleeping on now? The one you just told us is comfortable?' The Engineer and I were feeling a bit confused by the turn of the conversation.

'Oh,' he said. Just 'oh'.

Weirdly, the conversation left me feeling as if I was in the wrong and that no one believed we had bought a new bed for our son. I had become the mother who had not provided for her child. To the world, his word was more credible than mine, and worse: I could understand why people believed him. He was so believable whereas, I suspected, I was showing more and more signs of becoming unhinged. I had migraines every two weeks, I had developed an unknown allergy, I was exhausted and couldn't sleep. In an ironic twist, I'd started to mimic my children's behaviour by isolating myself like Isaak and being quick to anger like Miguel. Who would you believe?

Miguel was equally believable. One day we were at a restaurant waiting for my family to show up. We were mid-argument when they arrived. Miguel transitioned from attack dog to angel in a heartbeat. His harsh face and dagger eyes softened as he smiled and greeted everyone. Then he turned to me and showed an interest in what I was saying and smiled at me while he filled my glass with water. The performance was maintained until the meal ended and everyone went home. Then the steel door came crashing down. The soft look reverted to one of accusation.

When I saw my family the next day, everyone commented on how sweet and considerate Miguel was towards me. I could not make them understand that he had only behaved that way because they were with us. I tried to explain that we had been in the middle of an argument, but my explanation just didn't land. It made it worse.

'When I argue with my children, they don't make sure that I have enough to drink. I would love to have an argument like yours!' I was told.

'Yes, I am lucky,' I said, resigned. In those moments, I felt my seclusion even more completely.

The Engineer did his best to keep me stable and the boys on track. The arguments we had at home would sometimes engulf us all and we'd land up in a screaming match of 'us and them'. Just like most families, sometimes we would swap sides and sometimes we would stand together, but frequently the Engineer's rejection from the kids was as solid as mine was. Usually we were the outsiders in our children's lives.

'I wish I could understand what goes on in the boys' minds when they push us away so completely. What do you think it is? After all these years together, I can't believe that it is still about not wanting to be a family,' I said one evening, leaning against the Engineer. 'I mean, we keep proving that we are here for the boys, but they just don't want to see it.'

'It's hard to tell. A lot happened before we knew them. So much was set. Sometimes I think it just becomes about them keeping the status quo. The important thing is to remember that they do it automatically. They don't hate us even on those days we think they do.' He always tried to make me feel better. I knew he was at as much of a loss as I was. After all this time, neither of us had been able to fathom out a better way of dealing with our sons.

Most days, respect was absent from our house. Our children seemed to lump this quality in the 'for other people' basket. At school, they learned about children's rights. Unfortunately, there wasn't much mention of the responsibilities that come with rights. Miguel focused on 'the right to an opinion'. Armed with this, it became his 'opinion' that homework needn't be done, or that rules needn't be followed, or even bus tickets paid for; but most people outside our family circle would never know this dual reality. This random selection of entitlements plagued the Engineer and I, as well as their teachers. We were desperately trying to give our sons a world full of opportunities, but they couldn't understand us, and we couldn't understand them.

There are usually a few reasons a person lies: to avoid getting into trouble, fear of what another might think of them or for personal gain. Too often, in our case, none of these reasons applied when we caught our boys trailing from the truth.

'I keep telling you that I'm not accusing you of stealing the clothes, Miguel. I'm asking where you got them.'

A few soft cotton T-shirts had materialised in Miguel's cupboard and he wouldn't give an explanation. I hadn't expected the conversation to turn into the interrogation it had become.

'And I keep telling you that you bought them. Why would I say you bought something for me if you had not?' he argued.

'Except that I didn't get these for you.'

By now he was screaming himself into an atomic tantrum and started to hyperventilate. 'I can't breathe now. See what you've done. I can't breathe.'

'You need to calm down,' I said gently. 'You are having a panic attack. Just breathe out slowly as much as you can and then take a slow breath in. Let's talk about this when you are in a better mood.' I knew it wouldn't be easy to bring the subject up later, but the answer was not worth this distress.

The next day, while he was at school, I snooped in his cupboard. First, I found even more new clothes and then I found a receipt showing he had paid cash. It didn't take me long to work out that he'd bought himself clothes with his birthday money. My friends told me their kids told fibs all the time, but none of them had ever said their child preferred to get into trouble with a lie when the truth was more acceptable.

I became focused on trying to understand the reason for this deceit, so one afternoon I found myself walking into the clothes shop. I handed the assistant the receipt. 'My son bought some clothes here the other day,' I said. 'He got some T-shirts and I think some –'

'This purchase looks familiar,' the assistant interrupted. 'Oh wait, is your son Miguel? He's such a lovely boy. Always so polite when he comes in to buy clothes.'

I tried to look at the story from various angles, but I could not fathom what he stood to gain from these lies. All I could come up with was that being unable to trust meant that perhaps my sons both measured situations using a different ruler. It was as if Miguel *wanted* me to think the worst of him. He *wanted* me to reject him, but then he was disappointed in me if I didn't look behind his lie.

I had learnt that when a child skips a developmental stage, they come back to it later when it is safe. Miguel had skipped many milestones while he was trying to keep himself safe, including the notorious 'terrible twos'. A two-year-old tantrum is not quite the same when expressed through twelve-year-old lungs. And it can be quite overwhelming for all concerned. Understanding what is going on doesn't make it any easier to witness.

I felt as though Miguel was actively trying to keep me at bay, and whenever the wall between us came down he furiously rebuilt it, adding bits of glass and barbed wire on top so that no trust could break out or break in. I couldn't help taking it on as a manifestation of my failure to make my child feel secure.

I didn't need anyone to tell me that the less exposure to an institution, the better chance the child has of living an easy life. When we embarked on the adoption process, we knew that managing the effects of the environment the boys had grown up in would be extremely hard work, but we didn't know that it might be too late to overcome these ingrained behavioural patterns. We hadn't understood that their survival behaviours were already so deeply etched in their psyches. Miguel had turned to aggression and verbal violence to overcome adversity, whereas Isaak had turned in on himself, using adrenalin and instinct to guide him. These habits became automatic.

We were trapped in a circle of mistrust and duality, but the Engineer and I continued to live in hope. The only problem was, for the most part, hope began to seem like madness.

CHAPTER 32

Hard Work Makes Dreams Come True

At twelve, my boys still looked forward to the school swimming carnival. Miguel and Isaak left home wearing their school house colours and singing their school house songs. When they came home at the end of the day, Isaak showed me the ribbons he had won.

'I hadn't realised you were going to swim in the races today. Well done.'

'They said anyone could join in, so I did.'

'It looks like these were really big races. I'm impressed that you went up against some of those kids. I know that a few of them go surfing before school each day, and you beat them. Your swimming has come a long way, hasn't it?' I said warmly.

He didn't look very proud of his achievement. I could tell something was not right, but I assumed he was just tired.

Unfortunately, I learnt from his cousins that Isaak hadn't even jumped into the pool. Wishful thinking was still his preferred problem-solving technique. Isaak had come a long way since those days of being a beginner swimmer. There had been different levels of races where he might have had a chance of winning. He wanted so badly for us to see him as a winner, but he still didn't trust that we already did. He could not understand that he needed to do the work if he wanted to feel like a winner himself.

The boys were growing up fast and we kept hoping that home life would start to settle, but our lives just kept rushing headlong into a wall of distrust. At first, it was a few little things. Miguel kept reverting to his aggressive and belligerent ways. You could not teach him anything he didn't want to know because he hated feeling that he was not good at something. It made him feel vulnerable, and he had learnt that being vulnerable was dangerous and tantamount to the death of his personality.

People are learning all the time, but a child learns the most; and a lot of what they learn is not necessarily what they want to learn. Regrettably for Miguel, even when someone has natural talent, they still need to practise. But if Miguel didn't get something right, he would look for someone to blame.

There were times when I was able to teach the boys something new and equally as often I had to show them again and again.

'What's that smell in the kitchen?' I asked as I came into the house.

'Miguel and I were warming something up in the oven,' Isaak told me.

'But it smells like plastic is burning,' I said, confused.

'Yes, the Tupperware melted,' he said nonchalantly.

'But the Tupperware is plastic. How come you didn't put the food into an ovenproof dish?' I had shown the boys which dishes were good for the oven a dozen times.

'I always use the Tupperware,' Isaak said convincingly.

'But, sweetie, we've never had a microwave, so you can't have used the plastic tubs. You use the glass dishes.'

'Do I?'

My sons were able to learn and forget any number of things depending on what was going on in their heads at the time. Whether it was cooking or cleaning out the cat box, or even learning how to close a window, they were often determined to unlearn the lesson. Even if it meant their food would be inedible.

Homework started to become a big problem yet again. The boys would tell me that it was complete, and I expected the school to discipline them if it wasn't; but the teachers would constantly let me know that they had missed the deadlines and then leave it in my hands. I would do my best to make sure that Miguel and Isaak did their homework, but the school wanted the boys to take on the responsibility for themselves, even as they expected me to act as the disciplinarian. I started to get more and more emails from the school. The rusted-on habit of the boys leaning on conflict to move through life had made a comeback. Exasperated, I went to the school psychologist to ask for advice.

'I think you expect too much from your sons,' Dr Misterpsychologist told me. He was caring. He wasn't judgemental or mean-spirited like Señora SchoolPsycho. 'I've spoken to the boys,' he continued, 'and they are finding the work is too hard.'

'At times, I've been told by people who don't know my sons that I overestimate them, but I have a realistic idea of what they are capable of and don't set the bar high. Our situation is unusual, and I know it may seem that way to an outsider but that is not what's happening here,' I said, becoming annoyed. 'I'm not pushing for an A on tests. I'm simply trying to ensure the completion of a small amount of homework. *Some* work rather than absolutely no work. *Some* responsibility rather than none. It is not about their ability, but the idea that they don't accept that work needs to be done to learn.' Once again, I felt my explanation was letting me down. I didn't have the right words to lay out what the problem was.

'Have you thought about the fact that your boys might not be able to do the homework?' Dr Misterpsychologist asked kindly.

'I'm not even trying to get them to do it without mistakes. It is not that they *can't* do anything – it's that they don't even *try* to do anything,' I said. 'They spend more effort avoiding the work than the simplest attempt might take. I don't mind if they do something and fail. I just want them to try and put a small effort in. In the orphanage, if the kids didn't want to do homework, the volunteers would help move their writing hand for them.' I explained that some of them hadn't even learnt to hold the pen because some expat with a good heart would do it for them.

'I hear what you are saying,' Dr Misterpsychologist said noncommittally. I could see he still hadn't fully internalised what I was telling him.

'I wasn't a good student at school, so I know school is not for everyone, but I worry that they don't even try,' I continued. 'What makes it harder is that when the work isn't done, the school calls on me to set things right. Then the boys think *I'm* picking on them.' I wasn't sure who to be more frustrated with, the school system or my children. 'I'll tell you what. If you can find some way to test their level and it turns out that you are right, I'll gladly leave them to fail every test and not do any homework.' I hoped he would take up my challenge. 'But then, similarly, I will expect the school not to contact me every time work hasn't been handed in.'

Dr Misterpsychologist wanted to help. He arranged a test.

Three weeks later, I got a call. 'I've got an update on our conversation from last month,' the psychologist said. 'It turns out the boys are ahead of the class in both reading and maths. They appear to be quite capable. I apologise for my misunderstanding.'

I should have been content, but I wasn't. He still couldn't advise me on how to handle the situation. Miguel and Isaak persisted in not studying. The school continued to contact me about their missed deadlines. It continued to be an added stress in a family that still hadn't become accustomed to bonding with each other. I tried to get used to this 'new' normal but, of course, I couldn't.

In order to do something, you often have to first learn it and then practise it. And once you've acquired the skill, you can enjoy it. I wanted my sons to experience the feeling of a job well done. Apart from the usual parental disquiet about my children's academic future, I was also concerned that my boys would not develop persistence and determination. I wanted them to learn the cause and effect of effort and ability. Honestly, I would have been happy to simply see them *put in an effort* to become good at anything, academic or otherwise.

My voice was getting hoarse from nagging my sons. My brain was hurting from trying to be creative in this area, and my heart was sore trying to beat to the regular rhythm of my life.

CHAPTER 33

In Theory

'How long you been with the boys?' the young counsellor asked, holding his Styrofoam cup of milky coffee.

'They're thirteen now, so it's been about six or seven years.' We had ten minutes before Dr Neuro continued the presentation and I just wanted a few minutes to clear my head.

'I can't believe you're still having such problems,' he remarked. 'What have you been doing? By now, things should be sorted.' He sounded incredulous.

'Tell me,' I replied, trying to hold back a fierce response to the sting of his words, 'do you have kids of your own?'

'No.'

'In your counselling work, do you deal with kids from orphanages or foster care?'

'No.'

'I see. Well, nice talking to you but I think I have to get back to my seat now.'

'No, wait,' said the young counsellor as he accompanied me back to the seminar room, appearing not to notice that tears were pooling on my eyelashes. 'Maybe I can help you with your problems.'

The seminar was about bringing up kids like mine. Dr Neuro was an attachment disorder therapist, although he preferred the term developmental neuropsychologist. His special interest was post-institutionalised adoption – kids who were non-compliant or non-responsive. He was an amazing speaker and his poised, confident demeanour dominated the stage. That day, the presentation topic was Raising Damaged Adopted Children. His work was based on Romanian adoption issues that had started to surface.

In the past, people had been incredibly forthright about asking me questions or giving me advice. I even had a few people ask me, in front of my sons, if I wouldn't have preferred to have my 'own' children. Amazingly, they didn't seem to think this was intrusive or that my sons, whom they clearly saw as cast-offs, would understand. Some of these interrogators didn't even know my name.

'So do you know the boys' mother?' they'd ask.

'Of course, I know their mother. I see her every day in the mirror.' I would silently shout. 'We sit down to dinner with their father every night. Their aunts, uncles and grandmothers all take a keen interest in the boys. We know them all very well. Do your kids know their parents? Would I ask you if you'd wanted a girl instead of a boy while your child was sitting on your lap? No, the answer to all those questions is no, I wouldn't.' Those were the words I wanted to say, but instead, I'd plaster a smile on my face to hide my hurt. I wasn't used to people being sensitive to me, so when someone put a note in my postbox about this seminar, I wished I knew who to thank.

The workshop was for social workers and psychologists who often dealt with these 'problem' kids. The Engineer and I were the only parents there. One of the hardest things for me to hear was the presenter emphatically state that a carer was better than a parent for some of these kids. I had nodded when Dr Neuro said that sometimes a person looking after such children must do the impossible. I had understood when he explained that sometimes, during a full-blown tantrum, you might need to sit on them to rein them in. As much as I didn't want to do this, I could see where he was coming from, but I immediately rejected the idea that a carer was better than a parent.

'I'm sorry,' I interjected, 'but I can't agree that these kids need a carer more than they need a parent. We adopted our children at six. It's true that we're in constant strife, and we're continuously putting out fires, but we love our sons. I believe a child's primary need is love. We just have to be strong and patient. Why can't we love them like a parent while caring for our two boys?' I was feeling strong in my conviction and weak in my ability.

'The trauma and life lessons a child experiences in the first few years of life sets or breaks so much of a child's psyche,' Dr Neuro explained. 'A baby is born with all their receptors open, and in the first two years of life, they learn to attach. Their experiences in those years often determine how they will behave later in life. It is not about genetics, but rather epigenetics. This is the time when nurture will have the greatest effect on them. The baby will look for something to focus on – some love, a hug, a kindness or softness. If they don't get it, or worse, if they are abused, it becomes very difficult and sometimes impossible for them to learn to attach later in life.'

Dr Neuro went on. 'Experience has shown that even when a child finds a loving family after abuse, if they are older than four or five, they will not know how to find a comfortable way to show attachment and they will often not do it. The epigenetics make it so that the environment becomes more important than their nature or their genetics. Generally, the terms of endearment that go along with parenting don't coincide with what is needed in these situations.' Dr Neuro gave a sad smile and concluded, 'Attachment disorder is a tricky thing to live with on both sides of the problem.' He seemed to be talking about both my boys and I felt the familiar pang in my heart that signalled I was not working hard enough to fix things. 'It is very difficult to reverse,' Dr Neuro added. 'I sincerely wish you luck.'

At that time I had no idea that our attempts to parent our way through the challenges would bring us to within an inch of our sanity. What I still felt we needed was direction. We felt we were failing and that if we could only get the right guidance, the boys would be all right. Instead, we heard that we should not be doing this at all. The Engineer and I felt totally deflated. We knew we were beaten. We had gone to the seminar hoping for some advice and what we were hearing was not helpful. I just didn't understand what Dr Neuro was saying. To be honest, though, it was too late to see things differently anyway.

We knew that even before we officially became a family, we always thought of ourselves as one. Like most parents, we were constantly searching for more effective ways to deal with our children, and although we had not yet found the winning combination, we would never stop trying. No matter how long it took or even how close I got to breaking point, I would keep searching for the magical answer to help my children.

CHAPTER 34

My Brother's Keeper

From the first moment I saw Miguel and Isaak sit down in that hot and sticky homework room nine years earlier, I could see they had forged a bond through the fires of institutionalised life. They were the glue that solidified a puzzle of four. Three-year-old Juan looked up to Isaak. Isaak and Miguel leant on each to get through their struggles, while Miguel admired nine-year-old Angel. They all looked after each other, yet they didn't bond – close and yet not close in a kid-against-kid type of world. Through it all, Miguel and Isaak were each other's rescuers. It didn't matter if Miguel was saving Isaak or if Isaak was saving Miguel, they stood strong. Beholden and unbeholden to each other in the same breath. Whether it was calling for help when one of them got burnt by the water tank's open flame or stopping a bully from causing a physical fight or, worse, an abuser from doing the unthinkable, they would put themselves in harm's way for each other.

When I was a little girl, my mother would play a game with me. 'Lovey, something feels odd on my cheek.' Her eyes would glisten with a smile. I knew it was a trap and I couldn't wait to fall for it. 'What does it feel like? Is it sticky?'

'I don't know. Just put your finger there and tell me.'

I'd tentatively reach out a skinny finger, moving slowly to draw out the game. Closer and closer until I felt her soft skin. I'd push a little harder just as I made contact, just in case she missed the cue, but she never did. All at once, she would make a soft munching sound and turn her head quickly to pop my finger in her mouth.

'*Hm-mm-mm*, such a tasty little girl. I could eat you all up.'

I would let out a shrill squeal as I giggled.

'Again. Do it again.' I always begged for more.

It was such a delicately sweet memory. I wanted to give my sons the same cheerful feeling so one day, soon after we became a family, I initiated the game with Isaak. It was a mistake. The moment Isaak's little finger landed on my lips, he let out a shriek, but it was one of terror. He thought I was going to put his little finger in my mouth and bite it.

'No, mi corazón, don't be scared. It's a game. I just kiss your fingers – that is all. Please don't be scared. I am so sorry.'

Miguel was furious. 'What is wrong with you?' he yelled at me, and I felt the burn of his chastisement. 'Why would you do that to him? Don't you dare bite Isaak. Come away, Isaak.'

I tried to explain the game, but neither boy would listen. The gig was up and a saviour had swooped in. It was hard for my heart not to feel broken over their reactions, but I also felt proud of Miguel for looking after his brother. They may have disagreements or knock each other's teeth out and be at odds with each other, but my children would do almost anything to protect each other from outsiders.

By the time Miguel and Isaak were fourteen, we introduced a family rule that cell phones and computers were not to be kept in the bedroom. While we couldn't control all their online activity, at least we could make sure that at night, the phones were out of the bedroom and give our sons a reasonable chance of having a good night's sleep. Each night we'd remind the boys to leave their phones in the kitchen.

When Miguel started coming up to me just before bedtime and

advertising that he was putting his phone away, I became suspicious – but I told myself to stop looking for the worst in him. I wanted to believe that as a young teenager he was trying to show me that he was maturing. I chastised myself for distrusting him. But then we received the phone bill. It was close to $300, and the charges were mostly racked up between bedtime and the wee hours of the morning, when the phone was supposedly in the kitchen. Miguel is a very sharp person who can work any system given time and inclination. His solution was to put his SIM card into an old phone. Nice, clean and simple.

After being hit with a second big bill, we gave him a prepay SIM. The prepay would have solved the bill-shock problem, but then he took his brother's SIM and swapped it with his own once he had spent the allocated amount. Even simpler. Isaak covered for him. He was happy to get into trouble to save his brother from the same fate.

We confronted Miguel. 'Miguel, your phone bill is a problem for us. We can't afford to pay for you to be on your phone the whole night and you need your sle –'

'I'm not on the phone. I don't do that anymore. It's not my phone. You can't blame me for Isaak's phone.'

'But you are using his SIM.'

'No, I'm not. You never believe me.'

'Miguel, we know that you swapped the SIMs and you are using Is –'

'I don't do that anymore. You changed my SIM so that I can't and now I don't. No one ever listens to me.'

'Please tr –'

'Geez, you just don't understand.' He stormed off, mumbling, and I heard his bedroom door slam. I was left wondering if he would ever outgrow the belief that I couldn't prove anything if he didn't admit it.

Isaak was torn. He certainly preferred not to be in trouble, but he also wanted to protect his brother, who was stubbornly arguing against all our proof. I thought back to an occasion three years earlier when I was trying to get Miguel to study for a test.

'How can you see me texting when I'm not?' he shouted as his little fingers raced across the phone's keyboard.

'Miguel, I can see you typing on your phone under the glass table.'

Some days he was either so convincing or so aggressive that I would wonder if I was hallucinating.

'He's just holding the phone. He's not typing.' Isaak suddenly surfaced from his usual quiet self to protect his brother.

All children have a naughty streak and it is gratifying when siblings protect each other. I only wished my children would see that I was standing on their side too.

CHAPTER 35
Oh Child of Mine

One afternoon it occurred to me that once again, Isaak was not with us mentally. He was sitting next to me and I could smell his fourteen-year-old, testosterone-filled body. His torn fingernails were bleeding at the tips. I realised that he had not been present for quite a few days. He had become so adept at his disappearing act that I'd almost not noticed.

I knew I couldn't talk to him directly. He'd just morph into an alternate character if he thought he was under the microscope. I had to approach him from a different angle. I needed to show him that he was safe but under threat, allowing him to feel the comfort of risk. Coming from a point of danger was the key to talking to him, and this was the challenge.

'Isaak, I know how difficult things have been for you in the past. You have come so far and been so brave. The Engineer and I are so proud of you.'

He gave me a fake happy zombie smile. I knew this wouldn't work. I tried a new tactic.

'Isaak, I've noticed that you have fallen into yourself and I'm wondering what's going on?'

This time I got a morose and gloomy look. This too was going nowhere. Then I took a moment to bind my heart, close my eyes and find a stern voice. 'Isaak, what the hell is going on with you? You have been gone for days, and I am done with this. If you don't tell me what is going on, so help me …'

It was the last try. I couldn't attempt more than three approaches in one sitting.

My son Isaak has an affiliation with threes. You can try three times to get into his brain. If you find something that works, it'll work for three days, three weeks or three months. Even if he is enjoying doing something which boosts his confidence, he will only ever stick to it for a maximum of three months. Thereafter, the reset button is hit, and we have to find a new way of moving forward again.

That day I was lucky. The third try worked. He looked at me with clear brown eyes, and with no malice at all, he reached into my chest and tore out the remainder of my heart. Bandages, splints and all.

'I still miss my mother,' he said without spite.

He wasn't telling me that I wasn't good enough to be his mother, as his brother so often implied. He wasn't saying that he didn't appreciate me. It wasn't about me at all. I didn't even exist in that space. To him, she would always come first. That's what made it so hard and hurtful because his loyalty would never be reciprocated. When he was found wandering around a dangerous part of Mexico City at the age of about three years, there were no reports of a missing child. No one came to claim him. He had been completely overlooked.

'Isaak, sweetie, I can only imagine how challenging it is for you not knowing about that part of your own life.'

He sighed and bit hard on the ends of his fingers.

'When a person has an unknown background, it can make life hard. Maybe we can try to look at things differently.'

To survive his difficult start in life, Isaak found solace in creating a memory for himself. When he was in the orphanage, volunteers would take the kids to the park and play with them. He selected a picture of softness. A scene with a big green tree and a feeling of comfort with an inkling of safety. I'd heard him tell this story throughout the nine years we had been together. The details varied, but he always liked to describe the image he'd created. It's possible that he'd pinned his memory from one of those days. Or it may have come from a movie. It doesn't matter because most of all, it came from his heart.

'Maybe you can choose the park story as your base to begin,' I suggested. 'Or you can focus on the strength of the Mayans as your background. You can even make up something new. You get to decide what you want to be true for that part of your life and nobody can tell you that you are wrong.'

I let him hold on to his dream of a soft mother who had to walk away, but there was no way to discover the truth. Isaak's background was completely untraceable. For him, this was both a curse and a blessing.

'Not knowing is hard. I know it's not what you want,' I said, 'but you know, it also allows you to make up your own history. It lets you reinvent yourself as you go through your life.'

Isaak looked at me vacantly and carefully put a smile in place.

'Maybe it's a good idea to speak to someone else who is also adopted. Have you thought of talking to the Engineer? He also doesn't know about his biological parents.'

'Yeah, maybe I will.'

I got the feeling the conversation had gone as far as it would. 'You can always come and talk to me or the Engineer about how you feel. Whatever you feel is okay. You never have to worry about that.'

When the authorities had found Isaak, based on his stomach contents, they'd ascertained that he'd probably been eating dirt and junk for about three weeks. What I did not tell him was that some of the marks on his body had not been there when he was born. I could not tell him that, most likely, some very nasty things had happened to him while he was an infant lying awake, trying not to be a human being. Trying not to get hurt. Rather, I created mystical links that bound him to our family. All kinds of little coincidences, such as him sharing a birthdate with my sister, or having the same adventurous streak as the Engineer. I reframed any small connection to us as pre-ordained. I drew on all the allies I could muster as proof of our bonding so that he could unite with our tribe instead of being another abandoned kid. It wasn't difficult to find reasons to justify him being with us; I believed in all these small links myself.

Through the years, I strove for a solution so that my sons could find at least a semblance of harmony. Every day I did what I could. Conventionally, unconventionally, right and wrong, I kept at it day and night. Adding to my stress and depression was the fact that I never found a solution even though I did everything I could, searching books, documentaries and therapies. I'm not the academic in my family. Research doesn't come naturally to me. But this wasn't about me. It was about my kids. I knew it would help if I could work out why our boys often chose to shift towards the shadow instead of the light. There were simple and complex issues that I just couldn't fathom. I got sick and suffered carer's burnout, but I doggedly picked myself up and kept searching.

I began to understand that we were not alone in our inability to cope. I started to come across stories of disrupted adoptions. These are adoptions that go wrong and are terminated or annulled. Heartbreaking stories of kids being sent back to Russia from the United States or abandoned with notes saying that the new parents couldn't cope with the child's tantrums or other problems. We never once considered ending our relationship with our boys. Some of these stories described people who just couldn't bond with each other.

Bringing up kids with reactive attachment disorder is hard enough with love, let alone when parents can only find a general liking for the child. I cannot judge others harshly. It is not easy to love someone who doesn't want to be loved. Even when that someone is a child.

According to what I read, there is a ten per cent chance of a disrupted adoption if the child is aged between five and eight, and comes from an orphanage. Studies show that the longer a child can be kept in a family situation, the better. In contrast to this, if a child is neglected or abused early on in life, there is a high chance they will have long-lasting psychological issues. I couldn't help wondering what happens when a child remains in a family where they are neglected or abused. This happens often.

There is a huge amount of anxiety and depression amongst older adoptions, and if they have reactive attachment disorder, their chances at an easy life are smaller. Miguel and Isaak came to us from an orphanage at the age of six. I would ask myself frequently: what chance did our boys have of a happy life?

In their early formative years, our children, unlike other babies, never had the opportunity to learn to recognise a mother's voice or know her smell. They didn't learn the cause and effect that babies experience when they cry and are rewarded with food or hugs and kisses. Just like other babies, they learnt to judge their setting based on what they experienced in those early years. The pathways in their brains had been set. The abuse and neglect they'd suffered would always hinder advancement, leading to a closing down of the desire to learn.

My brave sons learnt from their early surroundings that to let their guard down would lead to their destruction. For them, the kindness and trust I took for granted did not equal safety or comfort. It brought them a feeling of disquiet. They had to work hard to find a new kind of normal in their lives.

In our case, although the love may not have been reciprocal, we were and still are a family. The Engineer and I had fought with all our might to bring our children into our lives. We'd had many opportunities to walk away when the officials in Mexico told us we could not adopt. We could have taken the easy way out. But we had not turned away. Through all our epic stories and mind-bending troubles, we had never had even the slightest inclination to pause, rethink and send our children back. I fully understand why some people at their wits' end land up at this unfortunate decision, but in our case, it was never an option we would ever consider. For us, Miguel and Isaak were our kids from before we even knew we would adopt them, and they will remain our kids no matter what.

Sitting with my son Isaak, hearing him verbalise a longing for a mother he never had, I tried to guide him into the light. I desperately wanted him to find peace. All I could do was help him hold on to the only softness he perceived he had ever known. My feelings and my knowledge would not aid him but maybe the memory of being in a fictitious park would.

CHAPTER 36

Fire Fire

Even though the Engineer and I had learnt to deal with Miguel's issues more effectively, we started to feel like we were slipping backwards. When he decided to look for an argument, there was nowhere to run, and even if we dodged all the obstacles he'd put in our path, the Engineer and I would still find ourselves in a full-blown fight with him, having entered into it via some unseen back door. I made sense of it by telling myself that due to his early-life trauma, he didn't want anyone to get too close.

The continuous fighting at home brought me to what felt like a final edge. I had not had much of a break from the time of meeting my children until this fifteen-year-old hubris. As happens with most parents occasionally, I believed I was due for a holiday. The reprive came from a very unlikely place. The Engineer's mid-winter staff party was taking place during a long weekend in New Zealand. The boys were going to sleep at a friend, and we were going to drink champagne with the Kiwis. I was looking forward to some adult, non-threatening, life-affirming company. That was until Friday morning when Miguel woke up with a high temperature. He just sat on the bed with no energy to do anything but stare at the floor. I realised it was serious.

Off we went to the doctor. When he told me that my son had bronchitis, I had no choice but to cancel the sleepover and my trip. Isaak went off to school, Miguel went to bed, and I went to the kitchen to make chicken soup. I am a Jewish mother after all.

The Engineer arranged to cut his trip short, but as his taxi pulled off, I thought I detected a look of guilty pleasure on his face. He didn't want to leave me behind but at least one of us was getting out alive that weekend. As usual, my car was parked just behind the Engineer's, which was in front of our house. I knew I would not be moving it until Monday.

When the Engineer returned home on Saturday night at about 9pm, he brought with him a conciliatory movie. The boys were asleep. Miguel had finally broken his high temperature and was showing some signs of recovery. All was peaceful as I sat down to watch the movie and instantly fell asleep.

'Wake up. Something is burning!' It was about 11pm. 'I'm going to check that the kids didn't go to sleep with a heater on,' the Engineer said, jumping to his feet and rushing for the red kitchen fire extinguisher before I could absorb his words.

I got up and followed him around the house. 'Are you sure it's in the house?' I said. 'I can smell some smoke as I walk past the front door.' By now I was fully alert. As the Engineer pried open the front door, I peered over his shoulder. The hue of a beautiful sunset was emanating from the road. The Engineer looked towards the road, then he looked at his miniature fire extinguisher and back at the road. 'Yeah, this isn't going to do it.'

I pushed past him and saw both our cars on fire.

'Umm, my car, and my husband's car ...' I fell silent for a moment while I grappled with reality, 'are *on fire*.' I told the North Bondi Fire Department.

'Okay, we have your address here and we're dispatching a truck now,' the disembodied voice said calmly.

'Umm, things are starting to explode.' I was still in disbelief. Surely cars only get burnt in the movies?

'Yes, well, that will happen if your car is on fire.'

'Oh. Yes, of course. What should I do?'

'Stay away from the fire.'

Good advice. I only wished I could use it in my regular life. As abstract as it sounds, I watched the flames licking our cars that June night with the casual acceptance of someone who has lived in interesting times. This incident was just one more in a series of strange events that marked us as different.

By dawn, the Fire Department had put out the fires. The police had interviewed me. The neighbours had prattled on about how high the flames had been. The tow truck had trundled away with both our cars, along with my sunglasses and my favourite CD. The kind lady from across the road had even brought out a broom and swept some of the ashes away.

Later we learned what had happened. A furious mother had shut down a teenage party gone wild due to too much alcohol and a penchant for fire. On their way home, the teens continued with their drunken fun. With alcohol-fuelled judgement, they didn't consider that throwing a flaming brown paper bag under my car would successfully set my Mazda 2 alight. They also didn't think it would release the burnt brake line holding my car in place and cause it to roll into the Engineer's car. With one careless throw, both our cars became tinder.

In one weekend, I had dealt with a sick child and lost two cars. My exhausted brain swelled with a bizarre pride: at least *my* kids weren't juvenile delinquents setting fire to property. That must mean I was doing something right.

CHAPTER 37

Trapped

'We're calling to ask if you know where Miguel is.' I was in the middle of a customer-service issue when the call came in from school.

'Actually, Miguel is at school. It's Isaak who is not. People often get them confused,' I said. I was used to the mix-up: the brothers were in the same class at school and the same team for soccer on the weekend. 'Isaak is at the excursion with the rest of his art class. I signed the slip. Did he forget to hand it in?'

'No, we know where Isaak is. It is Miguel who is nowhere to be seen. He didn't make it in today.' The voice on the other line was clear and determined.

'Miguel caught the bus into school today,' I said, equally determined. 'He left before I did.'

'Well, I'll check with some of his friends, and maybe you can call him and see where he is.'

My Australian mind told me, 'Don't worry, mate. He's just bludging school.' The Mexican in me said he'd been abducted, and the South African in me said he was dead, killed for his phone.

Mexico, with all its history and glory and tragedy, was a place where abductions were commonplace. When we'd lived there, people were regularly kidnapped and held until their money was depleted from an ATM. At the time, the crime was considered an assault, not a kidnapping. In South Africa, I knew people who had been affected by petty crime that had escalated to murder. I took a calming breath and tried calling my dear boy. I got no answer.

The previous evening Miguel had said to me, 'Tomorrow I have to be at school at the same time as you need to drop Isaak at the art centre.'

'Yes,' I'd said. 'I'll drop him off a bit early, so there isn't a problem.'

'Well, how about I catch the school bus in?' Miguel suggested. 'It's no problem for me. I don't mind. We did it last month when you had that meeting, and it was easy.'

The Engineer was somewhere in the world, but it was not Sydney. He would be no help dropping the boys off this time. The smallest alarm chimed in the back of my head, but once again I told myself to stop being suspicious. I carried on making dinner and tried to think nothing further of it.

The following morning, before we'd even had breakfast, Miguel asked not once but twice, 'What time are you leaving the house?' The alarm in my head increased in volume but I told myself that he was demonstrating independence, and an awareness that life didn't revolve around him.

SMS to Miguel:

YOU ARE NOT IN TROUBLE
BUT YOU DO NEED TO CONTACT
ME SO THAT I KNOW YOU ARE SAFE.
I KNOW YOU ARE NOT AT SCHOOL

Moments after I sent the text, I got a call from Miguel's phone. I wasn't sure it was him; all I could hear was sobbing.

'Miguel, where are you? Are you okay?' I asked him softly, but again, all I heard was more sobbing.

My colleagues at the other end of the office could hear me begin to yell down the phone line. 'Are you okay? Speak to me! Is everything okay? Where are you now? Are you *okay*?' People were converging in the doorway to see what a meltdown looked like, but all I could hear was solid crying. I was relieved when Miguel finally admitted that he was safely at home. I could stop imagining the worst. He had gone to the park until I left for work and then returned home.

Earlier that year, a mine had collapsed in Chile. The international press followed this story closely. Thirty-three entombed miners were trapped for sixty-nine days and were scheduled to be rescued on the day Miguel happened to take his day off.

Miguel had a lovely morning in the park and a quiet day at home playing games and watching movies. He sat comfortably on the couch and watched as the miners were rescued one by one. The well-publicised rescue wasn't his motivation for dumping a day of school. Although his teacher interpreted this as his reason for staying home – and he was happy for her to believe that – watching the rescue on TV was just one of the things he did at home that day.

Going AWOL from school was a minor offence, fairly trivial in the scheme of things. The true problem revealed itself the next day when Miguel and I were sitting in the vice-principal's office, talking to her and two other teachers. Mrs Helpmyson was a caring and loving teacher who had been assigned to assist Miguel and Isaak keep up with their schoolwork. Still, I had mixed feelings about her. She certainly wanted the best for my boys, but at the same time I felt that she didn't grasp my sons' unusual lack of ambition.

Like many institutionalised kids, my children had developed a much-needed defence mechanism. Their way of protecting themselves was to live in the present. Living in the moment means there is no future to worry about. But without a future, you can't have ambition.

I thought back on a conversation I'd had with Mrs Helpmyson just the week before. I had been preoccupied with the boys' future when we'd bumped into each other at the school pick-up. In her nurturing way, she'd stopped to chat. She had an idea of their background, and she was trying to ease my mind.

'What is it that makes you fear for your boys?' she asked, resting a soft hand on my shoulder.

'Well, off the top of my head, I know they are capable of doing so many things. But with their refusal to even attempt schoolwork, they may only have the opportunity to become street-sweepers,' I said as truthfully as I could. A lot of my stress came from the Engineer and me attempting to open doors for our sons while they insisted on slamming them shut.

'But there's nothing wrong with being a street-sweeper,' she countered with a smile that was meant to reassure me. 'I have so much respect for the sweepers in my street.'

I tensed up. 'Please don't get me wrong,' I said. 'I don't look down on manual labour. It's just that they are capable of more.' Like any parent, I wanted more for these kids who had been through so much trauma. My gut feeling was that I shouldn't point my children towards the lowest possible target and say – 'There you are – go fetch yourself that life.'

Sitting in the vice-principal's office, dealing with the fallout of Miguel taking a day off school, Mrs Helpmyson made the misplaced assumption that Chile, being in Latin America, was close enough to Mexico to be the same culture.

'Miguel, I think you feel connected to the trapped miners from Latin America, and you wanted to see that your people were safe.'

With the false cultural appropriation, she'd made a mistake that would give me something to think about for quite some time. We had heard that a lot of children who were the product of a cross-cultural adoption had identity issues. They didn't know where they belonged and so they looked for any connection to things that were even similar to their original roots. Thankfully, in our case, it was the only thing that I felt confident we had succeeded in. We had made sure that both Miguel and Isaak didn't have cross-cultural adoption problems. It was the least of our worries and I often took for granted the one accomplishment we could claim.

Miguel knew that he was Mexican and not Chilean, but he wasn't going to let that stop him from using this as an excuse. As he sat there, I could see the cogs working in Miguel's favour. Previously he had mentioned not doing maths homework, but now he had a better reason for being a no-show at school.

'We're talking to you as if you are an adult because you're sixteen years old, and at this age you can decide whether you want to be in school or not. The fact that you come to school every day shows me that you want to be in school.'

I could see Miguel immediately brighten up. Now he had a reason for yesterday *and* an excuse for tomorrow. That night he approached us with a decision. 'I'm not looking for a big conversation,' he said. 'I've given it a lot of thought and I'm not going to school anymore,' he told me clearly and in no uncertain terms. His teacher had told him that he didn't need to go to school and he felt that I had hidden that from him.

I didn't feel the need to have a conversation about it either, thank you very much. I inhaled deeply and became a superhero. In my mind, I started off calmly with the Dirty Harry quote, 'You've got to ask yourself one question. "Do I feel lucky?" Well, do ya, punk?' But in truth, I wasn't that collected. Even so, I made it very clear. Speaking in low and slow tones, I said, 'Now you listen here. If you want to drop out of school, you need a trade. And until you have a trade in mind, you are right: there is no conversation to be had.' At this point, I found myself quoting my father, 'Furthermore, we all have choices in the world, but if you live "under my roof, you will follow my rules." Am I making myself clear?' I pictured my father nodding in approval as I used the words I had heard dozens of times. 'And what's more, you are right, there is not going to be a conversation about it. Dropping out of school is not on the table.'

Then I slowly walked away with a manic smile plastered on my face until I could collapse in my bathroom where no, I didn't feel lucky, punk. In fact, just shoot me. Shoot me now.

I would go to the ends of the earth for my kids, but the horizon of opportunity was coming up fast with just two years left of school. It was time for the kind of tough love that parents often dread. No doubt, a tsunami was coming, and there was no higher ground to run to. I was desperately trying to deal with my kids who had a very different life-view from me, but I wondered if I had enough imagination to show them how to live an everyday life. I was trying to equip them with the tools to live, but they took my offerings and threw them in the imaginary tool shed at the bottom of the garden, and then set it alight.

CHAPTER 38

Drink, Drank, Drunk

> SMS to the Engineer:
>
> SORRY WE DRANK AND WE'RE
> A BIT DRUNK

As we watched our millennials grow up, we anticipated they would face a lot of hurdles that we hadn't faced as kids; nevertheless, some things never change. Just like countless other kids, we expected that one day our boys would come home drunk. We were also keenly aware that how we dealt with the episode would have far-reaching implications for our future relationships with them.

> **SMS to Isaak:**
>
> ARE YOU OKAY TO COME TO THE CAR? OR DO YOU NEED TO BE CARRIED?

The boys were about to start their final school year and they were out celebrating. As the Engineer pulled up to the agreed pick-up spot, he began to receive odd text messages from Isaak. He had a very early appointment the following morning, so sleeping at a friend would make the timing tricky – yet that was what he kept asking for.

> **SMS to the Engineer:**
>
> CARRY

It didn't take the Engineer long to realise that the boys' friend had been texting coherently until the confession that they had been drinking. Their friend had tried his best to keep Miguel and Isaak out of what he thought would be trouble. The boys had made a few good friends at school who took it upon themselves to look after our wayward drunkards for the night. It was heart-warming to see that, through all the difficulties, Miguel and Isaak had managed to forge friendships with such lovely boys. It was a marker that gave us hope for our sons' future relationships.

Once the Engineer had rounded up our sons and the friends who needed a lift home, he steered Isaak to the car. Miguel was very talkative.

'I'm not that drunk, you know,' he slurred happily. 'I could do anything I want to right now. Because, you see, I'm not *that* drunk.'

The Engineer was amused. 'Can you walk in a straight line? Because you don't seem to be able to do that right now.'

They climbed into the car.

'Guys, I want you all to know that nobody is in trouble. I'm glad you didn't try to keep this a secret for too long. I always prefer honesty and safety over everything,' the Engineer said. 'I'm happy to pick up any of you guys – *any* of you – if you're ever in a bind. Safety always comes first.'

When they arrived home, I sat up and watched the drunken procession of two stumble past me. Isaak needed someone to guide him through the doorways and into the room. The Engineer helped him out of his clothes. Miguel came to chat with me. He stood over me, and as he swayed, he held up his two hands in submission.

'Okay, okay. No, wait, okay. I'm in trouble. I'm in trouble, I know, but wait, okay,' he slurred.

'Who said you are in trouble?' I asked, genuinely at ease with the spectacle I was watching.

'Well, I'm drunk, and I threw up two times,' he said. As he looked at the two fingers he was holding up, he swayed so perilously I began to worry that he would fall and hit his face on the coffee table. But he was not done yet. 'Yes, I threw up twice, but not on myself. Which is *veeerry* impressive,' he said, gesturing to his clean clothes.

'Miguel, I think you need to go to sleep,' I said. 'You are not in trouble but let's talk about this in the morning.'

'No, no, no. I can't go to sleep now. I may throw up in my sleep and drown.' At school, they had many talks about drug and alcohol abuse. Miguel began to give me the lecture he'd heard a few weeks before.

'I think you need some water and then a lot of sleep,' I told him. 'Lie on your side and we'll check on you through the night. If you want, the Engineer will stay in the room with you guys for a bit to make sure you are both okay.'

'You'll check up on us in the night?'

'Yes. You'll be okay.'

'Okay. Then I'll go to bed. Because I'm drunk, you know.'

Needless to say, both boys were subdued the next day, but both insisted they were feeling great and weren't suffering headaches. Their mouths said one thing, but their faces told a whole other hung-over story. This gave us a chance to discuss social drinking, and to give the boys some advice about parties, drugs and alcohol. We felt we'd opened a door, reminding them that we would not freak out in times of trouble. We wanted them to know they could lean on us. We knew they still found it difficult to believe in our support. We hoped that in time, they would see we were on their side and finally learn to trust us.

In many families, parents don't know their children, and children hardly ever fully know their parents. The Engineer and I tried to bring our kids up with honesty, and to teach them to think for themselves. As we tried to teach them about cultivating an 'inside voice', they found a use for an 'inside persona'. One just for us to see. It was impossible for us to always be aware of how much our children deceived us. We couldn't discern how they behaved when they went out with their friends, drinking and cavorting and setting goals we didn't know about. A lot of kids don't want their parents to know them and our kids were no different. Often, I'd remind myself that other kids kept secrets from their parents too. Although for us it was more pronounced. I thought back to how Isaak had hidden his abilities when he was a little boy learning to tell the time at school.

Isaak was a master at the digital clock. I could not trick him, but he had problems understanding the analogue face.

'Isaak is doing very nicely this term. We are teaching the kids how to tell the time with the digital and analogue clock,' said his teacher. She was always attentive to Isaak and was one of the few people who seemed to understand his subtle distinctions.

'Yes, we have been playing games with clocks at home. He is quite good,' the Engineer told her proudly.

'Well, he's very good with the digital clock. The analogue clock is a bit of a challenge for him, but he'll get there soon enough,' I said equally proudly of Isaak. He was really showing us how hard he was working.

'Um, you mean the digital clock. He needs help with the digital clock,' his teacher corrected as she pulled out some work they had done in class.

'No, he knows the digital clock,' the Engineer and I said in unison.

Isaak's teacher shook her head at us and laid his classwork down in front of us. Each time he had to use the digital clock he got it wrong in class, yet at home, he got it right. At school, he was a master of the analogue clock. His self-preservation had told him that he should show his teacher one truth and his parents another. Between the teacher, the Engineer and I, we could see a full picture of his abilities; but on our own, we would never know this child. Such was the example of our child's inside persona. At school one thing, at home another.

Children of any age get a misaligned inkling that they will disappoint their parents if … and so they show us who they *think* we want them to be. This thinking can be dangerously flawed, in that it can make a bad situation worse. This secrecy also prevents parents from ever truly knowing who our children want to be. My children didn't want us to know their public persona. Perhaps they thought it didn't match our concept of a good person, or perhaps they used it as a way to keep us at arm's length. We would never know.

Some parents suspect they are losing their kids, and some find they have already lost them. In our case, I'm not sure we ever had them. And we kept on losing them. We were just being whipped along like pieces of paper in the wind.

Our children never came home drunk again, but experience taught us that this would not be the last risky behaviour. The Engineer and I were grateful that this time our story was similar to those that played out in other households around the world. There were no underlying reasons, no covert layers relating to institutions or abuse or abandonment. This was simply a story of two teenage boys experimenting with alcohol. It was normal. It didn't mean that we were any less worried for the safety of our children, as any parent would be, but I was almost proud to share with my friends an episode we could all relate to.

CHAPTER 39

Future Shock

The Engineer and I had been parents for eleven years. Still our sons had not bonded with us. Calm days largely eluded our family, but when things were going wrong for the boys, they identified the Engineer and I as the fixers. They would employ us to put things right for them and we had to console ourselves with the idea that this was how the boys regarded us.

Most parents don't enjoy enforcing tough love and I was no different. I continually longed for a random hug or kiss from my children, but I had learnt to accept that expressing their affection would never flow naturally for them. I found myself in a self-induced coma of daily office work followed by constant arguments on the home front. This repetitive conflict seemed relentless and it wore me down.

If Miguel decided he wanted to quarrel, no matter how many times I contrived to avoid it, the incoming argument would eventually get me. I felt trapped, kidnapped into an existence of self-hate as I struggled to do my best but repeatedly found that my best was not good enough.

School was often used as an excuse for the discord in our house.

When we first arrived in Sydney, my sons had been ahead of the class, but it wasn't long before their knowledge stagnated and they quickly slipped behind. I couldn't help worrying, but I learnt not to discuss the topic with my friends.

'Don't worry. Kids don't like to fail,' I was told many times. But I knew that my children's situation was different from most. Failure didn't have the same stain to them. In their short lives, they had endured much worse than failure.

'You are too involved,' people said. But knowing that my sons' futures were at stake, I didn't know how *not* to be involved.

'You need to force them to sit down and work' was another piece of advice. It was difficult to explain that my boys were like Schrödinger's cat: unless you lifted the lid, you wouldn't know what was there. Time was passing, but I felt we were simply marking it, with no discernible signals of change or progress. A year went by, then two. Before we knew it, childhood had slipped away, but things were not getting better. Then all at once, we were in the last year of school.

My boys still suffered from having missed out on those crucial early developmental years.

Everything counts when a baby is born. They learn the lesson of cause and effect: crying to express hunger. Being fed lowers the stress hormone and elicits relief, which they remember. They remember prolonged periods of stress too. Similarly, a child's vocabulary is influenced by verbal stimulation in their early years. Teachers are already seeing the discrepancies by the time children are four years old. Each missed step makes it harder to catch up.

We were constantly trying to recover from missing developmental stages. The effort expended in gaining one stage meant that another was being delayed. I couldn't help wondering how badly the early traumas would impact on my sons' final years at school. Like most parents all over the world, whether from the slums of Delhi or high-society New York, we wanted the best for our children. We wanted our children to have the best opportunities in life so they could have quality choices in their futures. We wanted them to be able to choose whatever path they desired.

The end-of-school exams were fast approaching. Miguel still believed that if he could dream it, it would happen. That he didn't need to put in the work to get the high marks. Reality would fall in line for him. Isaak was not driven to work because he was still stuck in a lost childhood and had no ambition for the future. I feared that if my sons didn't put in any effort at this stage, they would close down their options for the future. It's often said that during school finals, someone in the house has to be stressed. In our case, the boys were having none of it. Stress became our mistress while the kids lived it up. The Engineer had to start working from home during study break to ensure that our boys did some revision – or at least pretended to. Every teacher in the school became invested in pushing my boys across the line.

'I will be okay. Stop hassling me,' Miguel said angrily.

'I think I'm on track,' Isaak would inform me, putting down his Xbox control just long enough to look at my neck, not even bothering to make the eye contact he knew he was supposed to attempt.

One day one of the teachers called me in a flap. 'I'm sure you can encourage the boys to do some extra revisions,' she said as I tried very hard not to laugh at her naivety.

Somehow the boys made it through the final exams and then the waiting began. The days came and went, and one day the results were posted in the papers. The boys were in no rush to receive their final scores, but the Engineer and I were thankful our school days were finally over. It was no surprise to us that the boys' marks were rather unremarkable but there were no do-overs required.

'You aren't going to tell the family our actual marks, are you?' Miguel asked me rather nonchalantly. I could tell he wasn't proud of his results.

'Well, I'm not going to make any announcements, if that's what you mean. But the whole of the state knows the results are being published today so they will probably all look out for them. We can't keep it a secret.'

'Yeah. Just as long as no one makes a big deal out of anything. I'm glad it's all over now,' he said as he walked off as if he didn't care.

'How do you feel about your results, Isaak?' I asked him. He'd been sitting quietly, and I was worried he would slip into himself again.

'I'm kind of disappointed, but I am also glad it is over,' he said, biting his thumbnail and looking at my knee. He still did not seem to realise that the work he put in to the exams would affect the outcome.

The boys had made it through the school system and been spat out the other side intact. I hoped that having each found an interest, one in business school and the other in a design course, their personal motivation would kick in. Parental love can only get a child so far. It was time for them to take on their own responsibilities.

Nina Simone was singing in my ear, 'It's a new dawn and a new day,' and she was feeling good. She may have been feeling good, but I was filled with apprehension. The future was here, and I feared that my children's options were running out. I could only hope that I had given them the tools to start living the lives they wanted. I couldn't wait to be extricated from their studies, and I cautiously began to dream of them building a new positive relationship with us – one that didn't revolve around school, homework and missed deadlines.

I have always known that my sons' strength was built from vulnerability. They are amongst the strongest people I know, and I will always admire them. I hoped that with the conflict of school behind us, they would see me in a different light, and perhaps even find something to admire.

CHAPTER 40
School's Out

'Our cards have been hacked again.' The Engineer was calling me late at night from Rwanda, and I wasn't sure I'd heard him properly.

'I thought we fixed that a few months ago,' I said sleepily.

'Again,' he clarified. 'Again, not still.'

'Oh,' I said and turned over on my side. 'Anyway, I really need to sleep. G'night.' I ended the call, deciding that I'd wait until the morning to decipher what the Engineer had wanted to tell me.

With daylight came the realisation that for the second time that year we would have to reorganise all our payments. It also meant that for the next few days I could not use an ATM.

Miguel was leaving the house much earlier than usual that day and he was looking very spiffy.

'Where are you going?' I asked him.

'I told you,' he snapped. 'My uni group arranged a trip to the wineries.'

I was struggling to keep track of three people's lives, and desperately trying to live just my own. I handed him my last bit of cash, a $50 note.

'This is just in case of emergencies,' I told him. 'It's all I have for a few days because our cards were hacked again.'

That night I got a text message from Miguel: *Gone out for dinner with friends.*

I hoped I wouldn't run out of petrol before Monday. I needed that emergency $50 that had 'gone out for dinner'. I drove on empty for most of Saturday morning and then borrowed petrol money from a colleague. By the time I got home, it was midday and Miguel was just waking up after his night out. I had found it embarrassing scrounging money from a friend and wanted him to understand the difference between 'emergency' and 'going for dinner'.

'I had to sponge money to pay for my petrol today,' I told him. 'Did you forget I had given you the $50 for emergencies only?'

'Oops.'

'Oops' was all I got, and I didn't have the energy to explain why 'oops' was not really the response I had been hoping for.

A couple of weeks later Miguel came into my room. 'I just got my first tax return. I got a whole chunk of money. Now I can return the money I borrowed from some friends.'

'Miguel, it's never a good idea to borrow from friends. If you needed money, you should have just asked me.'

'You should talk. Just the other day you borrowed money to put petrol in your car,' he said as he huffily walked out the room, mumbling to himself.

In our family, the lighter side of life was often enveloped in conflict. I had to constantly remind myself to look for the lighter side of life. Humour helped us surmount heartache. One of those comedies began one night after I'd said goodnight to Miguel. I got a call from his mobile phone number.

'I have your son's phone. I'll return it tomorrow at the school gym,' said a stranger's voice on the other end. Having lived in Mexico, I knew about ransoms, so I used my negotiator's voice to find out what this man wanted. I was about to tell him that I had a particular set of skills when he told me that he had taken his students to the park for football practice. He'd collected all the forgotten jumpers, shoes and phones, and was now dutifully calling 'home' to let the parents know about the missing items.

The only problem was, Miguel was no longer at school and, in fact, had never even attended *that* school. He had, however, been at the park that day.

The next morning I told Miguel how to recover his phone. I was confused when he became angry at the good Samaritan teacher who had 'stolen' his phone. Fed up with being shouted at, I left the house to get myself an ice cream. I took that as a win. Ice cream is always a win.

By week's end, the phone was safely back in Miguel's hands. The Engineer was still out of the country on business, so the three of us went out for brunch on Saturday. We went to a quaint café that served food and sold books, stationery and bags. As I sat there listening to the boys breathing, chewing and slurping, I realised I could do some recreational shopping instead. I told them to come down whenever they were ready. 'Please, guys, don't rush,' I stressed to them.

After a little while, the waitress came down and gave me Miguel's phone; it had been left on the table. I rolled my eyes. As she started back up the stairs, she noticed Miguel coming down with a scowl on his face. She walked straight up to him and said, 'Are you looking for your phone? I gave it to your girlfriend.'

Not only did Miguel not accept the role he'd played in almost losing his phone for the second time, but he also did not find it funny. He was livid. He made sure I knew just how furious he was as we walked back to the car. How could I not laugh at the two-act lost-phone-slapstick routine? I'd morphed from the wicked witch to the youthful girlfriend. I saw the humour in it and, like ice cream, humour was always a win.

We'd been navigating around conflict as best we could, and the unavoidable arguments were often over money. The conversation had started the previous year, just before Miguel left for his six-month internship at an island resort.

'When I come back, I think I'll move to my own place,' he informed me with a naivety that demonstrated he had no idea of the cost of apartments in Sydney.

'Well, I don't think you'll actually have enough money to keep yourself going for more than three months after you get back,' I explained. The Engineer and I didn't have the resources to support him in a separate unit. We had renovated our house to make it comfortable for four adults to share.

'Maybe I'll become a policeman,' he said as a way to drop the subject and probably to needle me at the same time. I just kept my eyes on the road. I wasn't a rookie anymore; by now I knew when I was being goaded.

Now, six months later, he had returned from the island and the conversation was revisited, twisting against me in a topsy-turvy logic. Knowing that he wanted to leave home, I was concerned that he was spending all his money instead of saving it to move out. Each day when he came home, I got hooked into an argument that went around in circles. He wanted to move out of our home but had no money, and it was my fault because, as he told the world, 'You said I can't move out. So I'll spend my money if I want to.'

'Okay, that's fine,' I said. 'But then you definitely won't be able to move out.' I couldn't help stating the obvious.

'I'm leaving home because I hate living in this house. I'm never going to take anything from you again,' he exploded.

I didn't want to prolong the argument by pointing out that he was taking for granted the board, lodging, medical care, safety and warmth we provided.

'How will you move out if you have no money?' I asked incredulously.

'It is none of your business what I do with my money. I hate it here. It's your fault I have no money. I can't stay here. I want to move out.'

'Okay, so move out.' Just like the broom discussion in London, I was trying to make sense of the circular argument. Leaving home can be difficult for any child. I also knew that for Miguel, this milestone might be more complicated. He had made a home for himself against his better judgement. He wanted to be independent but had not yet developed the tools to support himself.

'I can't. I have no money,' he accused.

I was tired. I was sick. I was trapped in a life of anger and abuse that by now flowed in both directions. Some days I would drive past my house and just keep going until the sea stopped me, preferring to be amongst strangers rather than at home.

'I'll have one scoop of the passion fruit ice cream in a cone, please,' I said to the lady at the beach stand. I was trying to be friendly, but as I made eye contact with her, my face just couldn't pull off a smile.

'Here you go, sweetie,' she said, putting the cone in my hand. 'You all right, love?'

I handed her my money. 'Oh, yes, thanks,' I replied. 'I've just had a long day.' I turned away before she could see the tears in my eyes. If she had been rude to me I would have been better equipped, but her softness was the thing that undid me. The Engineer had been away for two weeks and she was the first person who'd been kind to me since he'd left.

I savoured the quiet moment watching the sea as I ate the ice cream with a zen-like focus. My energy had been used up, but I had to get home and make dinner. I liked arriving home after work with a sunny disposition so that the afternoon would at least have a good start. But more and more, I was finding it hard not to get caught up in the arguments that flew my way. Lately the Engineer had been travelling more than usual and it felt like the sky had landed on my shoulders. I booked an appointment with my therapist.

'I've been waking up in the middle of the night with a monster sitting on my chest, squashing the life out of my lungs,' I told her with a quivering voice. 'My stomach is always in a churn these days.' Tears hovered on my eyelashes.

'It sounds like you feel under attack. Is it more than usual?' she asked.

'Well, I'd hoped that after school the boys would be more settled, but Isaak seems to need more help than ever before. He's started forgetting to do the most basic things and I need to double-check everything he does.'

'How are things with Miguel these days?'

'Miguel seems more aggressive than he has ever been. I think he needs his independence but is too afraid of change to take it. It may be time to liberate us all from his tyranny but we've had so little time together.' Miguel kept insisting that we – or, more specifically, me – had 'made life a misery and was the reason for his downfall'. I felt Miguel was holding me to ransom.

'How are your headaches?'

'My migraines have started up every two weeks again,' I said. I also had a constant neurotic cough and I couldn't even look at food anymore, but I didn't feel like bringing any of that up. I knew I was burnt out.

'Are you ready to deal with the fact that you may be in a depression?' she asked gently.

'I may be depressed, but who has time to deal with that? Besides, when did anyone say that happiness is a human right?' I argued.

I left her office in a sulk with my human rights in a tissue box and my depression stuffed into the bottom of my bag.

To my surprise, when I looked at myself in the mirror, I looked normal. Younger than my age and certainly younger than I felt. I should have resembled a twisted crone from a Grimm Brothers' tale and yet there I was, smiling and fooling everyone that I was okay. 'Don't judge me by my looks!' I wanted to shout to the world. 'I am not okay, okay?'

The situation at home became even more untenable. No one was comfortable in the house. Miguel would come and go as he wished, leaving disharmony in his wake. I decided to help him gain his freedom for his sake as much as my own.

When someone goes out on their own, they often learn to become the person they can be. By contrast, when they live with a parent, they must accommodate someone else's agenda and expectations. Miguel needed to find his own way – either to make it on his own or understand how life worked if he couldn't. We would remain available to him, but it was time he learnt that responsibility comes from *doing*, not from dreaming. Miguel clearly understood that he had rights and yet he didn't want to commit to some of the associated responsibilities. He even scorned the benefit of paid meals and the safety of the family household. His planned escape was a setting free, just as much as a letting go. Understanding that once again the early start in his life was affecting Miguel's behaviour didn't help. I knew that the trust issues and delayed developmental stages all could have added to the bitter views my son had, but I was utterly exhausted. I had done my best. There was nothing more I could do if he thought it wasn't enough.

'Miguel, you are unhappy here,' I said to him one day. 'I know you want to move out, but you don't have enough money for a deposit. I've spoken to the Engineer, and we will help you move out. Choose a date when you want to move. We'll give you the deposit and the first month's rent. We can't do much more than that, but at least it is a start.'

'I will move out on the 1st of December,' he said before storming off, muttering under his breath that he was out of there. I thought he'd be elated but what he did next took me by surprise. He quit his part-time job. I wasn't sure whether to laugh or just head for a very high cliff as he declared in no uncertain terms, 'You made me so miserable that I can't focus at work.'

'You worked at a hotel serving people in the food and beverage department. I didn't think you needed that much concentration to bring coffee to people at breakfast,' I replied, unable to contain my disbelief. 'I thought you'd be happy now that you've been released from my authoritarianism.'

'You make me miserable. I had to quit.'

'But, Miguel, how will you move in December? Now you won't have any money at all.'

'I'll manage – it's none of your business what I do anyway.'

This record was not new; it had gone platinum. I had strong hopes that if he moved out, we might be able to save our soured relationship; but the date came and went, with the same repetition and manipulation. It became clear that he was afraid to leave but he needed to take the plunge.

I was worn down. It had become harder to find anything to laugh at. I felt that I had lost the fight. I had nothing more to give and I just kept hoping for a straw to float by so that I could grab it.

CHAPTER 41

Winning and Losing

Isaak was still not taking responsibility for himself. When we left him to find his own way of doing things, he began to sink. With his disinterest in his own life, I began to see that he might never take charge in his own life. He was still trapped in his early developmental misfortunes. Although we'd managed to arrange some special learning care with the design course he was doing, he was not coping well. Once again it fell on me to keep him going. He continued to see his speech therapist who would happily step beyond the expectations of her job description to help him stay on even ground, but he was not taking control of his own reins. I began to worry even more.

'Isaak, have you been going to all your design classes?' I asked him, already knowing the answer.

'Yes,' he said, almost believing his own lie.

'But I have a message from your tutors saying that you are not handing in your projects. If you are finding it too hard, you need to let the helpers know that you need their assistance. That's what we arranged for you. I hear you've missed a few of the meetings with them too.' Would

I ever escape the role of being Isaak's homework enforcer? I wondered.

'I'm not finding it hard,' Isaak answered. 'I'll contact them in the morning.' He gave me one of his sweet smiles. 'Do you need help with dinner?' he asked, deflecting the conversation. I didn't need help in the kitchen, but I let him help me just to have the contact with him. We stood together chopping veggies in his preferred state – silence.

I have been told many times that Isaak was highly functional. Ironically, the very use of the term in a clinical context comes with the understanding that help is needed. While he was capable of many things, there were also too many that posed a significant challenge to him. Compounding this was his total lack of motivation to do anything that might improve his situation. He could handle difficult situations and would know what to do in natural catastrophes or when things were at their most dire. But his day-to-day life was still disastrous. His room often reeked of old hidden food. He would forget to look after his hygiene and he would still need reminding about family chores which he'd had since he was six years old. Like his brother, there were some leftover developmental milestones that were still being caught up, but his processing had remained a hurdle. I had always believed that if Isaak wanted to get over that hump, all it would take was a small amount of effort, but he refused to do the little things that were needed to overcome them. He would overlook something as undemanding as taking vitamins. Reminders in his diary, Post-it Notes on the walls or even alarms set on his phone, it didn't matter what we tried; Isaak found a way to look right through all these and continue on his merry way, heading straight to the lowest form of achievement possible.

I began to worry that if something happened to the Engineer and me, Isaak would be lost in the world with nobody fully understanding what he needed. I had found a community care group who agreed to take his case on. They understood that he was not able to live an unassisted life even though he seemed capable to most onlookers. These professionals helped people with varying degrees of disabilities and I thought they might be able to help Isaak. Their first prescription was to have an occupational therapist assess the situation and provide a baseline.

'It's funny that you mention an OT because we have tried everything that an OT would suggest, and nothing has worked. His speech therapist has been very helpful in that area,' I said, trying not to sound too negative on the first round of phone calls.

'Well, that is good. Although there is a difference between a speech therapist and an OT, so I suggest we try an OT and see how that goes.' The voice on the other end of the phone was caring but firm. I knew that she had her job to do and if I wanted her help then I would need to follow the steps laid out in front of me.

'Okay, I will give it a try,' I said a little too convincingly.

I could hear the smile in her voice as she continued the conversation. 'You never know,' she said. 'The OT may come up with the perfect plan or something that you just didn't think of. If you want help, then this is the way to go.'

She gave me Ms OT's details and I called the next day. She came and assessed. She went and regrouped and reassessed. She spoke to all the people in Isaak's life I had put her in touch with. Hours and hours of assessing.

'I am sorry,' said Ms OT. 'You have tried all the things I would have suggested. In my report, I make note that you have tried some things that should have worked. There is nothing I can add. Nothing worked.' She sounded beaten.

'I need some help,' I said. 'Please – anything you can think of.'

'I am sorry. You have gone the distance. This is a first for me. I will only charge you for the hours I was with your son. There is nothing I can do.'

'I am worried that the care group will not take on Isaak's case without your help,' I whined to her, once again feeling the lump in my throat, knowing that my not-so-little boy had been disadvantaged long before I met him. I still felt like I was letting him down.

'I've sent my report to them,' she said, 'and they understand the situation. They have a better idea of what they are dealing with now and they'll continue from here. I just don't have anything new to add to your son's regime.'

I put down the phone dejected, but in a strange way, there was a relief hiding in the back room. I was vindicated but there was no victory. I had truly tried everything. I had come across the finish line. I had won. I had lost.

CHAPTER 42

After Holiday Blues

After a two-week holiday, the Engineer stayed on for work while I returned home alone. I flew home with a migraine and a stomach bug. My welcome home was icy which, to be honest, wasn't unexpected. I felt the message loud and clear: *You who are about to enter here, do so at your own peril.* Except I wasn't a trespasser. I was the proprietor, wasn't I?

'You never listen to me,' Miguel said as our argument spiralled out of control.

'I hear what you are saying. But I'm not feeling well and don't have the energy for this. I came home to find the house reeks of dog urine and neither of you guys noticed. Now I need you to help clean it up for me,' I said.

'Why can't Isaak help?'

'Because all I need is for one person to sprinkle the wooden floor with bicarb. It's probably too late but either way, it only takes one person. I need Isaak to help me with something else.' The discussion had become a childish competition. Neither of us felt heard.

'It's not my fault the dog had an accident. Why are you blaming me?'

'I'm not blaming you. I keep telling you I need your help. You aren't listening to what I am saying either.' My sense of reason was obliterated.

The boys had been left alone to fend for themselves for two short weeks. No harm had come to them, the animals were alive, and the house hadn't fallen down. To Miguel and Isaak, that was proof that they no longer needed me or the Engineer in their lives. To me, the truth was different – the dog hadn't been outside for a walk (in fact, I wasn't sure if the animals had even been fed every day), the food I had cooked before our trip had begun to rot in the fridge (I wasn't even sure the boys had eaten every day), and the wooden floors had been damaged and the carpet ruined. In less than two weeks, the bathroom had turned black with mould. None of this was life threatening but I could only imagine what would've happened if we'd been away for longer. Try as I might to get out of this circular discussion, my shouting match with Miguel escalated. I found it hard to keep track of what we were arguing about.

This argument was not new. It was just more of the same. It was about control and trust and help and kindness. It was like all the arguments that had gone before it. I felt that anything that had gone wrong before and after meeting my children was being pushed in my face. I was put in my place by an angry child who did not want help and did not want to help me either.

The memory of Miguel's last statement just before he slammed the front door as he left the house rang in my ears. 'I didn't need you to survive before and I don't need you to survive now.' Everything that I had done to help my children as well as what I hadn't been able to do didn't matter. It was used against me. The therapy, the lack of therapy. The advice, opportunities and guidance I had worked so hard to give my children was twisted as if it had been a plan to dominate and control them. I found myself swimming in a pool of confusion and self-doubt. After the argument, I began not to trust my memories and started to make a record of everything that was going on around me so that I could go back and reassess the situation when things had calmed down.

'The boys told me they don't know how to cook so I told them that next time they come to my place I'll show them how to cook spaghetti. They were both very excited,' my mother told me one day.

'Thanks, Ma, that's so kind of you. Although the boys were being polite. They know how to cook spaghetti. Maybe you can show them something new?' I liked the idea of them expanding their kitchen skills and spending more time with their grandmother all at once.

'Oh? But then why would they tell me they don't know how? Maybe they forgot. I'll show them an easy way when they come to me,' my mother said. 'They were so excited about learning to make spaghetti, so I'll show them how to do it again.'

'Well, they made some just the other day when I was late from work,' I said, feeling misunderstood and unheard. I had taught my children life skills and now I was feeling judged as a bad mother for not showing them one of the very things that I had taught them.

Isaak continued to ignore me in the most complete way. I was the ghost in the house. Miguel was so comprehensive in his anger and self-righteousness that after even a few minutes with him, I would lose all certainty of my recollections. I was waking up to the fact that I was alone and pondering the meaning of *my* reality. Miguel had told me I was not needed and not wanted in the house, and that I was the source of all his pain and suffering. This wasn't new. The difference now was: I was beginning to believe it.

From the time we met our children, the Engineer and I had focused on strengthening their sense of identity. We still ate Mexican food and celebrated that wonderful country. We had worked hard so that Miguel and Isaak did not have a cultural lack of identity. With so many cross-culturally adopted kids struggling to fit into their new backgrounds or feeling alienated from their birth culture, we made sure our children knew their past and future, and how they fitted in. My children didn't feel lost in their new world and also did not reject their Mexican heritage. At the time, I undervalued how important this success was.

Ironically, while effectively securing my sons' identity, I had finally lost my own and did not know how to find my way back into the real world. I had withdrawn from friends and family. The boys knew I was not well, but they couldn't really understand what that meant for me and they responded with indifference to any request.

'Just breathe,' I told myself aloud every day. 'Put one foot in front of the other and get through each moment as it comes.' I had reached the bottom of the ocean. All I wanted was to remain in the depths of the muffled sound. I had nothing more to give. I didn't know if I would be ready for any new surprises if they came along.

CHAPTER 43

Misconceptions and Other Realities

It was one of those hot Joburg summer days and I had taken my father's car to the corner shop to get milk. It was less than five minutes away on foot, but I had just passed my driver's licence and was keen to use it.

I paid for the milk and left. In the parking lot, I noticed how quiet it was as I got back in the car. I slowly reversed into the only other car there, which was still occupied by the driver and his children.

'Oh my goodness, I am so sorry. I'm sorry. Sorry, I just don't know, like, I'm just so sorry,' I declared in high-pitched panic. I was trying to remember what my parents had told me to do if I got into an accident.

'Calm down, lovey. Are you okay? I think you've had a big shock.' The driver unfolded his long, skinny, fifty-something-year-old body out of the car while his young children peered out, with fingers gripping the windows like Kilroy was there. 'We're all okay. It's just a slight dent in the car,' he said soothingly.

'Okay. Okay. Like, I don't know, I'm just, like, really sorry. I'm like, such an idiot.' I clearly had not calmed down yet.

'Lovey, when you get behind a wheel, you need to know that at some point, you are going to have an accident. My wife once took out a whole block of lights, so you see, you haven't done your worst. Let's just swap details and then you can go home and check with your parents if your car is okay.' He said this with such kindness that I wanted to hug him. I drove the two minutes home with care and a very shaky foot.

'Dad, I bashed a guy's car in the parking lot,' I said fearfully.

'Is anyone hurt?'

'No. But I dented his car.'

'Okay, later we'll report it at the police station so that we can put in the insurance claim.' My dad was repeating the conversation I had with my mother moments before.

'Why won't someone shout at me?' I cried, stamping my foot and storming off to my room to punish myself.

The man in the parking lot, my mother, my father – none of them had shouted at me. But I felt I deserved to be reprimanded. They all knew I was already punishing myself. That day I promised myself I would remember how my parents had dealt with me and I hoped I would be able to offer the same compassion and trust if I was ever a parent.

When we look back, the Engineer and I believe we did everything we could to show our boys we could be trusted and that we'd support them no matter what. Now, however, I can see that we were fated from the start never to be trusted. Their early teachings had cemented my boys into a permanent pattern that determined so much more than I could have ever comprehended.

In the final year of school, the boys applied for their learner's driving licence and they both passed. After finding out that they were the only kids learning on manual cars, they were not so excited. I was surprised that it became a daily struggle to get them behind the steering wheel because they were picking up the use of the gears very quickly. In the end, I gave up the struggle and waited for them to ask me. It didn't happen. When Isaak started his design course, the Engineer drove him in. After a while Isaak started to drive again. The Engineer often went camping with the boys and one trip, when the weather was not good for a few days, Isaak took advantage of a little town close by. He came home from that trip a new driver.

When Isaak passed his provisional driver's licence, we expected that the car would take a bit of a beating while he got the hang of parking. When he visited a friend and scraped our car on the wall of a low flowerbed, I was ready. It had not been a terrible crash. He had not been going fast and nobody was hurt. It was the second parking mishap within a few weeks. The first time he had tried to conceal the obvious scrapes along the side and front of the car. This time he called me straight away.

'The back door on the left-hand side is very damaged. The metal is broken,' he admitted. 'Do you want me to come home?' I could tell he was nervous.

'Is anyone hurt?' I asked, being careful not to sound judgemental. I didn't want to scare him into never setting foot on the pedal again. All that hard work of learning to drive would have been for nothing.

'No.'

'Is the wall damaged?'

'No, but the car is.'

'Okay, don't worry. If there is no damage to the property and no one is hurt, we'll deal with this later. Just send me a photo of what the car looks like and then go on with your day. We'll sort it out later,' I told him.

'Okay.'

'Okay. Have a nice day and don't worry about this. We'll deal with it together. No worries.' As I put down the phone, I felt that I had dealt with the situation well. I wasn't angry. From the pictures, I could see that the door would need to be replaced. I put that aside and went on with my day.

Later, Isaak came home with some of his friends.

'Hey, the next time Isaak visits you, please tell your wall not to jump out at him like that,' I said in an attempt at light humour.

'Sorry, that wall is a bad seed,' his friend joked.

We laughed and that was the end of the discussion. A few days later, I took the car in for a quote and, as expected, the door needed to be replaced. Knowing that Isaak felt bad about the door, I didn't involve him in the repairs because I didn't want him to feel any more pressure.

Although I didn't want him to be scared of driving, I was a bit worried that his next parking accident might involve a stationary car, so in the most matter of fact way I could, I told him to be a bit more careful when he parked. I also arranged another few driving lessons to focus on parking.

I didn't think about it further until a few weeks later when Isaak and I talked about trust again. I had caught him out in a porky-pie. It was something small, and I realised that the only reason he was lying to me was because he was afraid of my reaction.

'Isaak, haven't you learnt by now that I don't get mad when you make a mistake? I only get mad when you lie to me. How did I handle the situation when you damaged the car a few weeks ago?'

'Well,' he said, 'you were very angry and cross with me.'

Angry and cross. That was what he heard. That was what he felt.

No matter how I did things and no matter how I said things, his perception was always that I was angry and cross. I realised then that he would never see my love and my caring because to him, it just wasn't there. Even if it were written with a bright neon sign, he would never notice it. All he would ever see when he looked at me was the mother who is Angry and Cross. At every turn, I was reminded of the lost six years.

I could not be upset that my son saw me this way. His young life had started with a lesson in anger and abuse. Nevertheless, I couldn't help feeling hurt that he would always see me as a harsh person. It almost stopped me in my tracks. I had to remind myself to breathe, to pick myself up and remember that he had been the victim, not me.

Throughout my mothering of these boys, I've had a lot of time to think about all I've done wrong in trying to do right and to understand why my kids have rejected me so completely.

'Adoption runs in my family just like eye colour,' I joked one day in the doctor's rooms. And then I realised that in my family of four, I was the odd one out, being the only non-adopted person. A good proportion of my friends and extended family are adopted too. Some went scouring the world for their biological families, and some didn't. Of the ones who did go hunting, they seemed to divide into two groups: those who were curious and those who were looking for something better than what they had landed up with. Sure that fate had mistakenly placed them into the wrong spot, they went seeking their holy grail. Sadly, a few of these seekers found themselves on a 'search and self-destroy' mission. They did not fill the hole within themselves, and as a result, their hurt ran deeper. The past had happened to them when they were small, and at the time, a door to a new life had been irrevocably opened. They had been pushed through it, and now they found out that it had been one way. Some found their biological families but felt alienated from them. This made them experience abandonment twice over. Others found good friendships but no more. It was those who were merely curious who fared the best. They were not looking for a missing piece of themselves and were therefore not disappointed.

It seems to me that some adopted people feel they come from a void. Isaak fell into this group. I could understand this because as a non-adopted child, at times during a tantrum, I too wished for better than my given lot.

I imagine that as an adoptee, sometimes you have to make up your own story to survive because you wish you'd come from a prince or a princess who, for some important reason, could not keep you. You long to find them and live happily ever after. At least, this is what I suppose my truth might be if I was adopted.

I had a friend who was very successful in business yet unlucky in love. She would sit with a glass of rosé in her hand and tell me that she would be so much happier with a husband. One day I couldn't stop myself. 'You know, Linda, these days marriage is not a guarantee. You have to be happy within yourself. A man is not going to make you happy. Only *you* will make you happy. Not all marriages are good.'

'Yes,' she said, 'but I don't want one of those marriages. I want one of the good kind. One like yours.'

I think that sometimes adopted people can't see that if they'd stayed in their birth family, they might not have had 'one of those' perfect lives either. Each family has its issues. It is sad to realise that sometimes the past that went missing might be better off lost. I'm not talking about all adoptions, and I'm certainly not talking about forced adoptions, but it is a part of some stories. Some of my friends who are adopted only remember the 'ogre factor' – the times when tough love was used to help them or when their parents shouted or were tired. They blame their parents and may even come to hate them. They don't understand why Mum and Dad did what they did. They may remember standing on the side of the road being humiliated while a mother shouted at them, but won't remember that she was shouting at them not to run into the road.

This lack of understanding hurts all parents. All of us want our children to comprehend the reasons for our actions. We want our children to know we did our best. I think adoption adds an extra layer to a parent's fear. Will our child reject our love and never come back? Will they leave us one day, and not return?

Growing up, a child doesn't always know why something had to be one way or another; they just remember feeling unloved. They take this misunderstood memory into adulthood and hold on to it, forgetting that it was the exact love they craved that made the parent do what they did. This is *my* worry. This is *my* fear. This is *my* pain.

All I can do is hope that one day my children will remember some soft times we shared, and smile.

CHAPTER 44

Somewhere to Run

From the start of my parenting journey, I was aware of many obstacles in my path. Time had gone by all too fast and I was still struggling to bond with my children who were no longer little ones. Our family unit required resources that we could not find. We found ourselves leaning heavily on gut feelings and whatever I could glean from articles, books and therapists. Not being able to touch our child when he needed a hug the most, not knowing our children's early history and not being able to demonstrate acceptance were things that other families wouldn't find common. Our influences were different, and our successes depended on things that many families wouldn't have even needed to contemplate. Sometimes a win would come from the sidelines of our life. A hard fall being acknowledged. A trip on a bus or train where the boys led the way. A passport control officer being confused with our family dynamic while we stood together as one. Sometimes something as simple as me letting my children prepare their own dinner would go further than a show of love could. It felt as if my battle-weary family had been put together by Father Nature and Mother War.

As a mother, I had given everything for my little family, but there came a time when I needed to get out. In a twist of fate, the Engineer returned from a business trip and provided the solution. His company had opened up the opportunity for us to move to Mauritius. As I stood in front of the Engineer, he posed the familiar question: are we in or are we out?

I have always had an unconventional approach to decision-making. Either I vacillate for years trying to make the perfect decision, or I know my mind before I can even articulate it. I once spent nearly the whole day in a shop, driving the salesperson mad trying to decide between the red elegant cooking pot and the black bohemian one that looked like it belonged in a witch's lair. At times, the Engineer and I have appreciated there is no right or wrong decision. In the absence of extra information, we pick one direction and move towards it. This seemed like one of those times and I made up my mind immediately.

'Mauritius is warm. I hate the cold. Nobody knows me there. The boys will soon turn twenty-one *and* they can cook. We could leave the house to the animals and the children.' I excitedly ticked the points off my fingers. It took me seconds. I would find someone to oversee the goings on of the house and then I would move to my new home in Mauritius where I would try to heal. 'I'm in,' I said definitively.

It was a gamble, a zugzwang, but I feared that if I did not move, I would be inviting despair across my threshold indefinitely. To preserve my sanity, I had to take the chance. All my life I had tried to help people; but those to whom I was closest, and who needed me most, just doled out rejection. I had fumed and lamented, felt sorry for myself and ignored my depression, but now I had to save myself.

When I had the opportunity to leave my parents' home straight after school, I had grabbed it. Now I had my own grownup home with my own grownup kids who refused to grow up, and they didn't want to stay young either. I didn't understand my children's choices. By now I could see that at their age, they needed to take hold of their own lives.

Moving to Mauritius offered me the chance to find meaning in my life again. It was time to examine those inspirational sayings and charge them with meaning: *the walk away, hold my hand, soar like an eagle, drop out, take some quiet time* and *go be social* kind of cliché. Pop psychology told me that the way to happiness would be to walk away from those who hurt me. And I absolutely wanted to do that. It made sense to do that. The only catch was that I'd be walking away from my children who still needed me, even though they didn't realise it. I still felt the lioness instinct to protect them, and I would have ripped out your throat if you'd stepped towards them in malice. But I desperately needed some space between us. It was the only way to recover my stability. It was the only way to give our relationship a chance.

I felt as though I was running away from my family, my friends and even my job. Time moved slowly for me, and I hardly noticed the passing days. I wanted to move forward, and yet I had no strength to do anything but vaguely exist. I'd wake up and feel a sumo wrestler sitting on my chest. Easy breathing was foreign to me. My stomach was twisted, my shoulders were neurotically reaching up towards my ears while a highly-strung woman was banging her stiletto heel against the inside of my skull to get out. I was not doing well.

Broken, battered and bruised, I was an emotional vagabond; but I was not dead yet. I didn't know it at the time, but I would need every bit of my remaining endurance to get through one last encounter before I would be able to regroup in my new land.

CHAPTER 45

I'm Okay – You're Okay?

Two weeks before our flight to the paradise island was scheduled, sometime after 11pm, we got an unexpected phone call. And then it happened. The moment that any parent dreads when your child is in danger, and confusion and clarity fight to take control. Immediately followed by the rush to hospital. The tubes and pipes and oxygen attached to my child. My son. My Miguel. I stood outside myself as I watched a nurse bark orders to her colleague: 'Get him into resus B. Now! Leave the oxygen. He's going to crash.' She was directing her words to the nurse standing next to me, but I felt it's warning aimed at my own mother-heart.

The waiting. The dread. The *waiting*. I had always feared this. Now illogically, I worried that my terror had brought it on. Over the years I'd tried to convince myself that this would never happen. That we'd taught our children well and they would know better. Except he didn't. Miguel did not know better. As with all the trivial arguments that had come before, he thought he did. But he bloody well didn't.

He had indulged in risky behaviour which left him in a coma for close to twenty-five hours. The rest of us stayed as close to his side as the hospital would allow. Awake. Fretting. Pacing. And then the nurses sent us home.

Miguel woke up feeling refreshed and ready to share a funny story with his friends. The rest of us woke up exhausted but relieved that he was okay. Days later, he came home to a hero's welcome. Friends visited, and I was glad, thankful beyond words, that my child was unharmed. He'd made it through. But then I overheard him telling his friends where he went wrong and how he could have or would have been safe. As his confident voice drifted down the stairs, I became apprehensive; I couldn't trust that he wouldn't take more risks with his life and limb, and I'll be definite here – he was not safe. My fear told me he would never be safe. He had not learnt his lesson. To me, it didn't matter that he was almost twenty-one years old. To me, he was still my little boy, and I was still scared for him.

Miguel was still the king of secrets; and even though his life would have been far easier without these deceptions, he held on to this concealment, always maintaining his disguise, ensuring that only a couple of people really knew him. He still believed that in order to survive, he had to control his truth, ensuring that those around him would only know his camouflage. To the outside world, he appeared quiet, helpful and well mannered; at home, he was still full of rage and anger, stubborn and disrespectful. He seemed to scorn anything that was important to the rest of us. We found no consolation in understanding why he was the way he was. It didn't help that he was a child going through a difficult life. It didn't even help knowing that he felt comfortable enough with us to exhibit this behaviour. The comfort to act out is one of the biggest compliments a parent of damaged children can receive, but it is also counterproductive and the stress of living with this type of tribute is disheartening. In our case, it became more and more difficult to live with a person who wanted only conflict.

Our lives seemed to diminish with every passing day. The more I tried to help him, the worse things got. The more care I offered, the harder he looked for conflict. He would push, and push, and *push*. Eventually, when all my buttons had been pressed, I would explode. Sometimes I'd see an argument days before it arrived, but I could no longer keep my emotions contained. Instead, I'd find myself on the bathroom floor in tears, wondering how I could have landed in such an intractable situation.

To make matters worse, I felt unable to confide in my friends. When I did open up, they tried to convince me that Miguel's behaviour was typical; they'd tell me not to worry. But they had no idea what we had been going through. This miniature god of wrath had sent me into my deepest and darkest vortex of depression, trapping me beneath a dome of anger, frustration and resentment.

It felt as if for a few moments of fourteen years, I had had two sons. They had been small, and their situations had been big, intricate and somewhat thorny. When we adopted them, we knew that it wasn't going to be simple or even agreeable all the time; but still at one stage, we definitely had two sons. Sometime in that last year or so, I felt as if I'd lost one. I had *seen* the imminent train wreck, but I just couldn't get out of the way. It broke my heart and tore at my spirit, but I had to admit he'd been honest with me from the start, when at six years old, Miguel had looked up with those determined brown eyes and said, 'I don't want a mother.' At the time, I thought he was scared and that I could help him. Naively, I'd thought that love conquers all, but I'd forgotten that I had already learnt that love is *not* all you need. Love is not enough. Love is just love. No matter how much you try to heal a wounded person with love, you can only get so far.

I had told him that instead of being a mother, I could simply be his good friend. But I didn't realise that I was lying. I did need to be his mother. The alternative was to walk away, and I would *never* have walked away. How could I? He needed help, and I thought I could give it. Later I would describe it as a no-choice situation. I would tell people it was as if I had already walked onto the landmine. Although I was still whole, there was nothing I could have done to change the outcome. The booby trap would detonate the moment I lifted my foot, and I would be wounded no matter what I did. If I'd walked away at the beginning, I would have destroyed myself trying to work out what I should have done. Instead, I stayed. I fought for love, and I lost. So I say again: I thought I had two sons for a time, but if I'm truthful, perhaps they never really wanted to be my sons; and that broke me.

I found myself telling my story, sharing my pain and my grief, and I was given another kind prompt.

'It sounds like they need psychotherapy,' a friend suggested, trying to be helpful. We had only recently met, and my story was new to her.

'My god, thank you. I never thought of that,' I said, unable to contain my sarcasm. We laughed, but I wanted to hurt this lovely, kind and deeply caring woman. I wanted to hurt her because I could no longer take being the one in pain.

'I would really like to try brainstorm some ideas with you,' she said. 'I want to come up with something to help you.'

I softened again, basking in her genuine desire to help me. It wasn't that I resented the suggestion. It was just that I'd tried everything already. Incentives, punishment, rewards, focusing on the positive, therapy, holidays, computer programmes, New Age ideology, spirituality. Every helpful suggestion poked through me like a crude assegai. I could list every option we had tried and yet I always harboured the feeling that there was one more theory I should try so that everyone could get on their feet. Try again. Go back to something that worked once. Go back to something that may work now even though it didn't work then. Try. Try. Try. I think I can. I think I can. I think I can. But I just couldn't anymore.

I spoke to a trauma therapist – she on her mobile, me huddled quietly in a corner of my room, hoping my boys couldn't hear me.

'What exactly have you done about your children's trauma?' she asked.

My heart sank. It was beyond me to articulate everything I had tried over the phone in a ten-minute conversation. She switched the conversation to me.

'I think you have carer's burnout and need trauma counselling yourself.'

I heard her words and broke down. I had never had time for my own trauma counselling and now it felt too late – I had already drowned. I was just a ghost talking to a voice on the other end of a cell phone. I ended the call mumbling to myself about what I thought I knew about PTSD.

'My children are not my trauma,' I said loudly to the cat sitting by my feet. At the time, I did not understand the concept of carer's burnout. I didn't realise that all my physical ailments came from a place of stress. The constant worry and repressed emotions I experienced were at dangerous levels. The continuous fear for my children had taken me beyond the normal amount of parenting. I did not realise that I had my own PTSD going on and I underestimated what the trauma therapist was trying to tell me.

I took a deep breath and headed out of the house for a quiet walk as the tears fell down my face. I wondered if I would ever be good enough.

CHAPTER 46

Who Are Miguel and Isaak?

By the time I met Miguel and Isaak, the words 'family' and 'love' had been twisted to mean 'danger', 'abandonment' and 'abuse'. We had to choose our words carefully. Our children could not call me Mama, a word they associated with anguish. The Engineer could not be called Daddy because that would make him an accomplice to trauma. Those choices were stolen from us. We did not have the opportunity to name our children or even choose the words that named us. Instead, our children called us by our first names. Many people misunderstood and harangued us about this decision. As they got older, the boys occasionally held this against us, telling people they are not *allowed* to call us Mum and Dad. They didn't remember the repugnance generated by these words and that it was their choice to relinquish them. Once again, we couldn't align with the most basic normality. 'Come to Mum. Go to Dad.' It was just another difference we had to be strong about.

But even though our connection with our kids hasn't been an easy one, I can't say it hasn't been beneficial. Our sons are people who are worth knowing.

WHO ARE MIGUEL AND ISAAK?

At twenty-one years of age, Miguel has long skinny fingers and toes that fit his delicate frame. He is handsome, trendy, and always looks well-groomed. When he was a child, he loved running around in a pair of green tracksuit pants, as far away from the neat, smart young man he has become as you could get. He is always scented with aftershave. As a small boy, he didn't like his mischievous brown eyes. He wanted them to be blue. Blue would have been a lie, a cliché. Most of all, blue eyes would have made him someone else.

Miguel is full of contrasts. He is gentle with people he doesn't know, hiding an ancient rage that burns deep in his soul. Perhaps because we are identified as parents, and therefore are associated with his harder, early years, his anger peeks out in private. The fact that he does accept us as his parents means that we are privy to his fury. Only we are privileged enough to be burnt to a cinder by his temper. There is no small warning. No light glowing amber to caution us. With us, his setting goes from laid back to Bloody Sunday in six seconds flat.

Yet to say he is only that would be wrong. He is helpful and kind, and he shows a deep caring for anyone who is less fortunate. When he smiles at you, you feel the warmth his smile radiates. When people describe Miguel, one word is commonly used: sharp. They mean he is clever, shrewd, fast-minded; but I know it is also true for both meanings of the word. He is astute, and he can be cunning too; but when he releases his anger on us, it cuts deeply. It comes to him as naturally as does compassion when a beggar tells him their life story, or when a child talks about a teacher's injustice. Then he is soft, affectionate, loving.

He was broken very early on and reconstructed in a way that mutilated his spirit deeply. He has two personas and finds it difficult to allow anyone to get close; the risk is too great. It is difficult for him to let you see his vulnerabilities if he is not ready. He seems to have no choice but to stab at your heart. It isn't his fault. It is what he thinks he must do to survive.

Miguel can do anything he sets his mind to. He is good at all sports, often teaching himself the game. He is one of the most capable people I know; and yet he doesn't have the confidence to strive for more.

Where Miguel is slim, Isaak is stocky. At twenty-one, he's put on quite a bit of the Nutella on toast around his face and waist; nonetheless, he is still brawny. He sits hunched over intricate drawings that his clever fingers create. Dots and squiggles and fine lines become things of beauty as he creates worlds within worlds on paper. He is a Mayan, and like all Mayans, he is small of stature and strong of body. When he was six years old, he could lift the Engineer off the ground. He always looks handsome, with bright-coloured shirts against his dark skin, but habitually chooses to wear sweaters in the heat and short sleeves in the cold. He likes extremes of temperature against his skin.

After watching him over the years I noticed that when left to his own devices, Isaak would sit alone in a room and look back on his past, gaze into his future and stare into the void within. Whenever we can, the Engineer and I try to stop him from heading further into the depression that he can't help steeping himself in. We attempt to set tasks for him or suggest life skills to develop, but this compounds his conflicted existence because he just wants to do nothing but ruminate. Yet allowing him to indulge in this sends him deeper into his darkness and then he can't or won't do anything for himself. If we force him to 'live', he is only living the life that we have placed in front of him. When we show him the boxed-in reality he chooses to dwell in, he struggles against us, refusing to choose life. His solitude is his drug, and it is as harmful as heroin. He too believes he can stop anytime he wants.

His sense of humour is subtle and doesn't appear often, but when it does, you get a glimpse of a finely crafted mind. A gentle soul directs him. A helpful spirit lies within, but he is often lost in this world of doing and being. He comes alive in situations of conflict and danger. He is the person I would choose to follow out of a disaster. But his disaster, his misfortune, is that his life is no longer characterised by danger, so he is locked in this half-life, this stupor in which he parks himself.

Like Miguel, Isaak is excellent at all sports. When he runs, he's like a cheetah, unstoppable – here one moment and then he's gone. He is helpful and sweet and, most of all, he is kind. He will genuinely take the rougher path to make others' lives easier. I have seen him cheat so that someone else can win a game and feel good about themselves. Maybe one day, Isaak will find an inner peace and manage to achieve the success he deserves. He too has no idea of what he can do in life and, like Miguel, would be able to do so much more if he could just see what I can see.

Our ambition for both these boys has always been to show them they are loved and to help them cultivate trust in themselves and accept it from others. We did not to push them to be *the* best, but rather encouraged them to do *their* best.

Early on the Engineer and I realised that the life ahead of our boys would not be easy, and that regardless of what we did, it might not be enough. I feared that they wouldn't understand how much goodness I wanted for them. I often felt that they perceived me as the person standing between them and happiness, even as I sacrificed so much to try and bring it to them. We came to understand that without trust, it is very difficult to build a solid foundation and our boys would struggle to lean on us. We realised that helping them to stand strong on their own would be the next best thing to aim for even though, deep down, we always hoped they would learn to love us. Instead, we have had to settle for our mission being to teach them practical life skills and independence so they could forge a life on their own terms.

CHAPTER 47
Finding Myself

The dread that came with those few days of hospital visits didn't change our plans to move. It did however give me something extra to fear as we waved goodbye to the boys. I second-guessed our decision with each added kilometre that brought us closer towards the airport and yet another new homeland. But I was surer than ever that the last chance we had at a normal adult relationship with Miguel and Isaak would be improved with distance. And so, as the sun hit the tarmac and the plane took off, I had just enough energy to keep me moving forward.

Having planted and killed my second tomato bush (an unfortunate pastime that seems to happen every time I move to a new country), I stood in the garden and realised that I must be settling into my Mauritian abode. I noticed a struggling spider in our swimming pool and went to get the pool net. As I fished it out, I asked myself why I always bothered saving the arachnids. My dislike of them goes back to when my mother bought me a four-poster bed. I would often wake up at night with the hallway light coming into my room from the little window above the door. I'd admire the shadowed lace.

One night the pattern looked a bit different. A dark shadow looked at me from the middle of the fabric and then moved. In a panic, I reached for the torchlight and yelled out for my parents. It was a giant spider. The third time this happened, I became an arachnophobic maniac. Through the years I have moved up and down the scale of fear towards these silk-makers, but I have never fully conquered my fear of them. At times I have wilfully annihilated them, while at others I've run to the Engineer for salvation. He refuses to kill them, preferring to gently take them outside while I stand there shouting irrationally, 'Don't touch me until you have washed your hands!' So clearly, I care very little for these eight-legged creatures, and yet I find myself at the side of the pool each day, saving them because I know that sooner or later their spindly hydraulic legs will give out. My fear and dislike for them doesn't preclude me from saving the terrors.

I love most creatures that have fewer than eight legs, but my favourites are snakes, lizards and frogs. When we first moved into our tropical island house, I would often find a variety of these drowned in our swimming pool. The poor things had taken a moonlight swim and discovered that it was easier to jump in than to get out. I wanted to save them (as well as the dreaded spiders) from this common fate, so I consulted the Engineer. He didn't disappoint. His idea was simply a man-made lily pad in the man-made pond, and all it took was a tile of coloured foam. Reptile, mammal and spider alike now have a chance to save themselves.

When I was about eight or nine years old, I enjoyed helping in my parents' hardware store on Saturdays. I looked forward to the moment when my mother handed me the cream-coloured cloth bank bag with money in it disguised inside a shopping packet. Clara, the tea lady, would take my hand and together we'd go to the bank to deposit the shop's takings. I've never been sure how much money was in the bag, but in my little mind, I always imagined – lots and lots. It made me feel very grown up. But the other reason I loved these trips was because on the way back, Clara and I would stop off at a Chinese shop around the corner. It was there that I learnt about different cultures and discovered that there was not just one way to live a life. From then on, change and adaption became part of my world. In that tiny blue shop with a red door, I discovered Buddhism.

The more I learned about Buddha, the more I wanted to become enlightened. Before long, I was burning incense and telling my childish self not to worry about death, but rather how I treated people in my life. I didn't renounce my Jewish religion. Of course, at that age I didn't fully understand what Buddhism meant, but I held on to this interesting way of life.

In time, I learnt about Hinduism too, incorporating some of its wisdom into my own. I wasn't picking and choosing, I was taking the best aspects of them all. By the time I was twelve, I had absorbed pieces of every belief system and culture I came across: from African folklore to Zen Koans, from throwing the sangoma's bones to the I-Ching. I learnt everything I could. I stood for it all, and I absorbed everything that came my way. I was open to seeking the truth in different ideas and changing my ways as I went along.

I became aware of my tendency to casually help people. Picking up clues from those around me. Letting strangers know where to find the cheese in a supermarket or telling someone they were heading in the wrong direction at the traffic lights. One night in Sydney, I came home to find two drunk teenage girls wandering down my street. I didn't know them or their parents, but I drove them home.

'You're such a busybody,' my friend Linda said when I told her this story over coffee.

'How could I do anything differently?' I protested. 'What if I was the last person to see those girls alive? How would I face their families?'

She shrugged. 'Most people don't get murdered, you know. And besides, all this helping and saving will destroy you one day.' She bit into her pastry. 'You automatically swing into action to change, or do, or help. What do you get out of it?'

'There is no personal gain to it,' I said. 'It's just something I end up doing. To be honest, I don't give it much thought. To me, it seems natural that if someone needs something I can give, why wouldn't I give it? Isn't that what people do for each other? It costs me nothing to be kind.'

Linda had no answer.

In East Africa, I once helped an Italian family. I couldn't stop myself. I helped them, and then I slipped away. It's the underlying story of my life. Rescue and be gone. Protect and disappear.

I was sitting in a hotel lobby, watching the concierge packing suitcases onto a trolley. The Italian family to whom the cases belonged were leaving. You could see that in their minds, they were no longer in Africa, they had already arrived home. They were demanding and self-centred, rudely shouting and clicking their fingers at the concierge before sauntering off to wait in their air-conditioned stretch-limo.

The bags were being expertly packed onto the small trolley. All except one red bag that remained forgotten on the floor. The Italian came back to hurry things along. Off went trolley, bags and men, leaving just me and the red bag in the lobby. I watched 'Red' with mounting unease, trying to mind my own business. 'Nasty man should not have interfered. He deserves to arrive back home having left you in Africa,' I told the bag with a satisfied smile.

The concierge returned. He wiped his brow and I saw his shoulders visibly relax, ready to move on to the next task. I realised that even if the Italian with his slick black hair and snooty daughter and haughty wife did deserve what should have been coming to them, the world is not a fair place. The man in front of me would be blamed and might even lose his job.

'Samahani,' I said to him, 'that red bag belongs to the Italian family.'

'Asanti sana, you have saved me. Thank you very much,' he said.

I winked at him and walked off, knowing that I had saved a bad story twice.

Lost and semi-alone on our island, trying to heal and move on, I sat down with my sorrow. Slowly, I started to recognise all the times I have changed things along the way. Consciously accepting the responsibility sometimes brought unease because often I couldn't give assistance fast enough. People don't always want the help that might bring them peace because transformation can be arduous. I realised that I can't be a saviour to everybody. You see, I am not a saviour. I am just a changer, after all. A changer and adaptor. An adopter, if you will.

The Engineer and I had tried to give our children everything we thought they needed for the world, but we could only give what they were willing to receive. I will always be there when, or if, they decide they need or want me.

Other adoptive parents sometimes ask me how I coped. I try to explain that I didn't cope, I endured. I wasn't able to take away my children's obvious or hidden hurt. In the end, I was the one who had to accept that I was not able to unbreak them. I had kept trying to work on myself and my patience, technique or knowledge. I blamed myself constantly for not being good enough, not clever enough, not able enough. I had to accept that for me, the role of 'mother' came with a different job description than the typical mother. My boys' early childhood experiences turned out to be more tenacious and powerful than anything I could have imagined. I had to adjust to what would make them feel safe, even if it meant that I couldn't be the mother I wanted to be. Perhaps the gift I have received in return is that I have finally learned that it's okay to look after myself.

Looking back, I honestly believe that the quality of life we were able to give our boys was better than what they might have faced had we left them in the Mexican orphanage. We had hoped they would accept more from us and the opportunities we provided them, but as I have often said, 'You can lead a horse to water, but if you force them to drink, social services get called in.'

I still promote the ideal that love should have the opportunity to conquer all, but I could not save my children any more than I have. I realise that I am okay with being different from my friends and have begun to comprehend that I am happy on my own path, being true to myself. I had been trying to follow the mould of 'mother and family' and this sat heavily on my shoulders. There had been no group to offer us sanctuary. No 'come to us and we'll share our secrets'. No group therapy in which we might sit with awful coffee and dry biscuits, and nod and smile and say, 'Yes, us too. How about you?' Every day I woke up and told myself that maybe my best wasn't enough. Then again, maybe nobody could have done any better. What I do know is that when we found these boys, they were two of many in a place where everyone had to look out for themselves. Nobody had ever done anything for them. Not a thing. But then the Engineer and I came along, and we tried to make a difference. Although our family does not conform to expectations – either mine or others' – we still have a relationship. At least I can hold on to that tenuous thread.

In that year of change and sadness, I spent a lot of time alone. I didn't want to hear about other people having fun or loving their families. I couldn't face thinking my failure was so complete while other people went on with their happy lives. I just wanted to sit and stare, not even move, aside for a slight swaying of my body to the rhythm of my heartbeat. I did not want to wear a fake smile and hide my battered heart. That would mean that I needed to wear a happy *happy* demeanour so that others didn't feel the burden of my own oppression.

The Engineer's annual company party brought an unexpected comfort. There, in the middle of the fake opulence of Sun City, South Africa, I reconnected with my annual friends. Despite some of us being bigger or slimmer or greyer, most of our friendships were still as close as they had always been.

I couldn't hide from Tanya. She saw through my fake cheeriness and steered me to a corner to catch up. She was doing well. Her kids were growing and maturing and returning to human form after the teenage years. I broke down and couldn't hold back. I blurted it all out. My pain, my disappointment, my confusion – every part of my struggle gushed out while in the background, a Frenchman was aptly singing, 'Je ne sais plus. Je suis perdu.' I don't know anymore. I am lost.

As she sat there holding my hand and looking into my eyes, Tanya said, 'Have you grieved yet? You probably need time to grieve. You need time to grieve for the family you thought you had. For the family you held in your arms and loved and cared for. For the love you gave but which wasn't received.'

And there it was. The signs were all there, but I hadn't listened to the whispers. I hadn't grieved yet, and I wanted to. I really wanted to … but, you see … I thought she was wrong. You can't grieve for something you never had, can you? Yes, I wanted to cry and tear my clothes and dirty my face and sit on a bench and just grieve. But I couldn't. I didn't know how.

That day in Mauritius, standing next to my pool, net in hand, dried-out tomato bush behind me, I sat down and grieved. I grieved for myself, for the person I used to be. I grieved for my children and my family, and all that came before me. In grieving, I started to accept the positive changes I'd managed to make along the way, and I accepted that we had not left even the smallest opportunity unchecked. The Engineer and I had done all we possibly could do, and then had still found the strength to do more. There was nothing further we could have done for a better outcome.

I grieved and accepted, and then, somehow, the world turned for a moment and reset. There at the swimming pool, looking down at my imperfect reflection, I caught a glimpse of my old self. I started to see who and what I am. I called out my name. Not my given name or my chosen name, but the name of what I am. The sacred name that is hidden within my soul.

    Catalyst.

    Changer.

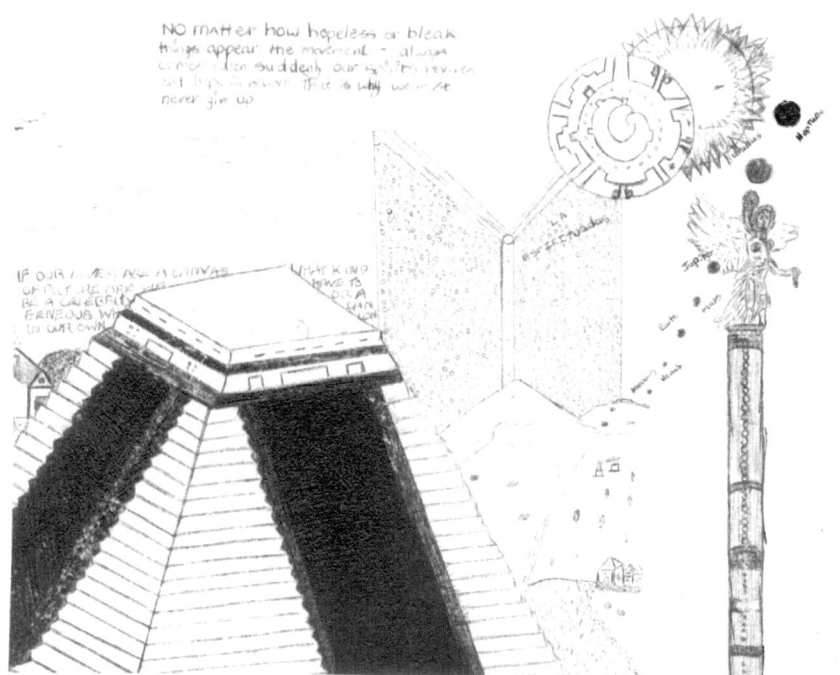

My Son's Thoughts After Reading the Book

I was adopted around the age of six or seven years old and, until a couple of years ago, I lived with my adoptive family. I am old enough to stand on my own feet now, and these are some of my thoughts relating to the topic.

What is my opinion on adoption?

I feel that people often think of adoption as a straightforward concept, and as a final and perfect solution for a lot of kids in orphanages, although my view on adoption is probably a little different due to my personal journey. I feel that adoption is a great thing and it should be encouraged *if* the right processes have been put in place. Adoptions can give an individual a second chance at life, but if the transition process is not handled correctly, it can culminate in long-term negative psychological issues which can cause a lot of additional problems in someone's life. It is for this reason that I feel adoption should not be viewed as a solution to fixing someone's life but rather a second chance at life. Even though I still think that in some cases, it is better to be put up for adoption, it's not as clear-cut as the concept is made out to be. A lot more thought needs to go into each individual adoption to help each family with their particular differences and challenges.

Not all orphanages are safe for the children they are supposed to be caring for. I came from an orphanage that was not the worst by far, but my friends and I did not get good care and we were not always in a safe environment. I know that there are different reasons people get adopted and I am focusing on the adoption circumstances that are similar to mine. I cannot talk about adoptions that happen because a birth parent doesn't have enough support and I am not talking about forced adoptions either. I can only talk about what I know.

What is my opinion on my personal adoption?

Even though I feel I have developed and overcome a lot of my traumas which were more related to my early childhood and events that happened during my time in the orphanage, I do feel that some of my traumas were caused by the adoption process. In principle, I feel the orphanage had a set structure in regard to the transition process of the adoption but due to limited time and lack of communication and organisation, it resulted in the process being sped up, and steps being missed. This in itself led to additional psychological issues which made settling in and bonding *very* challenging.

How do I feel the book will assist families touched by adoption?

I feel that the adoption process is often only focused on the transition as the final step of the process. But I think the transition process is just the start and that the following years are more important. A lot of families feel that adoption will be the happily ever after. It is usually more complicated and more complex than that. Adoptive families often feel lost as to why their particular adoption might not have run as smoothly as previously thought. Or they might think that other families are doing better than them.

MY SON'S THOUGHTS AFTER READING THE BOOK

I believe this book will give guidance and hope to families dealing with similar issues. It will let them see that they are not the only adoptive family having problems.

Note: Both my sons contributed to this book, each in their own way. They shared some ideas and thoughts as well as provided artwork. I have deliberately not mentioned which son did what in an attempt to keep their lives a bit more private.

Acknowledgements

I'd like to acknowledge life, the Universe, and everything, but then I would be plagiarising the wonderful Douglas Adams, may he rest in peace. So instead, I'll try to keep this brief – after all, you have just done a whole lot of reading.

I'd like to thank all those people who suggested I write a book, and then all those other people who listened to me droning on about it. John Stoke – thanks for being the first person to actually take your time to read the worst version of my draft. I can't thank you enough for not packing out laughing (at least not to my face) about all the creative spelling you had to wade through.

Thanks to my accountability buddy during the first stage of the book. You kept me on track and reminded me to get out the house sometimes. To my pod buddies – thanks for reading my first shitty draft and giving such careful feedback. Those wonderful women I met on writing retreats and workshops, who gave me advice, support, Facebook explanations and emotional support, you each were a hand at my back at times when I needed it (and sometimes when I didn't need it anyway).

Thank you, Norie Libradilla. Sorry about the hundreds of emails starting with, 'I know this is a silly question but …' You were always ready to hold my hand and give me encouragement. Thanks for all your proofreading too. I don't know how you do it. Nailia Minnebaeva, my cover designer, thanks for your patience, advice and all the extra artwork you provided for me. Thanks for an *awesome* cover. To my first editor ever, Nadine Davidoff, thank you for all your wonderful suggestions and feedback, and for working so quickly. You were kind and thoughtful, and you helped me bring out the best book I could write. To Alison Lowry, who did my final edit and still had to put up with my special grammar and punctuation, I am ever so grateful. Your generous comments gave me strength. Without you, this book wouldn't be what it is. To my friend, mentor and publisher Joanne Fedler – there are so many words (and I'm a writer now so I know a few of them) that I could say to you and they will never describe my gratitude. Seriously, some of my best breakthroughs you helped me achieve in the writing of my story were also my best breakthroughs in life. All I can say is simply, 'Thank you'.

I'd like to thank my mother and sisters who support me in most of my crazy endeavours and for being ready to pick up some of the pieces when things fall. And my mother-in-law who, still after all these years, has never uttered a harsh word against me.

To my children, you will never know how much of a hero I see in both of you. I hope one day you find peace. Thank you for encouraging me to write our story. I hope you are happy with the result. I am proud of both of you.

To the Engineer, I dream it and you create it for me. LyPb.

About the Author

Xanti was born in the late '60s and grew up in South Africa. As a little girl, she found out how powerful writing could be when her first-grade teacher asked the class to write an essay. Although it was well written, she learned that it wasn't a good idea to write about her teacher shouting all the time. After that, she was a lot more discerning about who saw her words. It took her another forty-five years to show her writing to anyone.

She started travelling at the age of fourteen and has lived in seven countries. She learned something new from each, which added to her eclectic lifestyle. After seeing the shadows and the light of abandonment and abuse, she adopted her two children. Her experiences as an adoptive mother shaped her view on parenting, childhood and everything else. She's been through earthquakes, volcano eruptions and a couple of fires.

Xanti has always been interested in the human psyche and understanding the reasons for why we do the things we do. She feels that making your own roots is more important than looking for meaning in those that came before us. She is committed to the planet and is a firm believer in equality for all.

You can visit her website at **www.xantibootcov.com**

www.ingramcontent.com/pod-product-compliance
Lightning Source LLC
Chambersburg PA
CBHW021057080526
44587CB00010B/274